WITHDRAWN

WORN, SOILED, OBSOLETE

Extraordinary Interiors

Extraordinary Interiors

Decorating with Architectural Salvage & Antiques

Brian D. Coleman

Photography by
Dan Mayers

Gibbs Smith, Publisher
Salt Lake City

First Edition
09 08 07 06 05   5 4 3 2 1

Text © 2005 Brian D. Coleman
Photographs © 2005 Dan Mayers

Published by
Gibbs Smith, Publisher
P.O. Box 667
Layton, Utah 84041

1.800.748.5439 orders
www.gibbs-smith.com

Designed by Dawn DeVries Sokol
Printed and bound in Hong Kong

Library of Congress Cataloging-in-Publication Data

Coleman, Brian D.
  Extraordinary Interiors : decorating with architectural salvage and
antiques / Brian D. Coleman ; photography by Dan Mayers.
      p. cm.
  ISBN 1-58685-435-6
 1. Decoration and ornament, Architectural, in interior decoration.
 2. Found objects (Art) in interior decoration. I. Mayers, Dan. II. Title.

NK2115.5.A73C65 2005
747—dc22
                                            2004025155

Contents

Acknowledgments

The author and photographer wish to thank first and foremost the staff of the architectural salvage store Olde Good Things. This book began after initial discussions with them and the majority of interiors were found with referrals from Haroldyne, Kevin and other Olde Good Things staff, who were always encouraging and willing to help. The homeowners in the book were uniformly welcoming and enthusiastic and allowed us to create such a beautiful book—thank you all. Madge Baird, our editor, was always supportive and reasonable, enviable qualities for anyone, especially an editor. Amy Tan introduced us to Mrs. Ann Getty, which led to our beautiful cover, and we wish to thank Amy for her interest in the book. Dan wishes to thank Misha, Lola and his parents for their support during his frequent travels, and Brian thanks Howard and the kids for their constant encouragement.

Reflections on Collecting

I am so proud that my Turkish Bedroom from our San Francisco residence is featured in this beautiful book. A reflection of my love for travel, it is a favorite of our guests, luring them back time and time again. Like the artists whose work is featured in the room—Delacroix, Matisse and Gerome—I am drawn to the visual impact of Turkish design. If one studies the art form, the interiors become deeply spiritual once you learn that the decorations and carvings have been created over a period of many years by dozens of hands, often as a form of meditation.

The room began in 1990. While traveling in Paris, my good friend Barbara Newsom called to tell me about the sale of a rare Turkish bedroom. I realized the eighteenth-century Syro Turkish window peltings, frames and panels would be a beautiful way to use architectural salvage in our home and immediately bought the entire room. Architectural salvage and antiques are a marriage made in heaven. The treasures of salvage used in our contemporary life is a way of continuing the traditions of the past, and its aesthetic of old-world craftsmanship has been an important tenet of my design projects.

My fondness of beautiful interiors and the joy of creating family spaces with treasured antiques come from my family home in Wheatland, California, and the extensive influence of my most significant mentor, J. Paul Getty. I have had the great pleasure to work with some of the most famous interior designers of our time. My special favorites were Sister Parrish and Albert Hadley. The teal library they created in my San Francisco home remains as they designed it and still feels wonderful all these years later.

Doris Duke used her Turkish rooms at Shangri La for entertaining. I use my Turkish room to delight the senses of my guests. My great thanks to our curator, Deborah Hatch, for tracking down the antiques in the room and working hard to preserve and improve our collection, and, of course, to Brian Coleman for recognizing the value of architectural salvage in our culture.

—Ann Getty

Introduction

Architectural salvage has a special beauty all of its own. The intricate turnings of a nineteenth-century carved-oak newel post from a Victorian mansion; the sparkling jewel tones of a stained-glass window from a razed church; the color and patina of crusty wrought-iron fence railing from an inner-city brownstone all share a charm and attention to detail that is rarely found today. Castoffs from another time, architectural details such as these are actually works of art on their own. Their pride of craftsmanship shines through, whether it's a roughly cut oak beam from a 200-year-old barn or a sophisticated glass-and-metal Art Deco chandelier from a 1930s movie palace. Saving and reusing these artifacts not only allows us to enjoy them once again but also preserves these treasures for future generations.

This book celebrates the beauty of architectural salvage and showcases distinctive homes and very personal spaces that have been transformed using common building elements from the past. We visit fascinating and unique projects across the country, from Soho to San Francisco. Homes include an 1820s brick warehouse near the seaport in New York City that was gutted and rebuilt using architectural salvage, including old wooden ceiling beams, flooring from a nineteenth-century dairy barn, and a soapstone kitchen sink with faucets cleverly operated by foot pedals from a hospital operating room. Or see how an early-twentieth-century barn in the softly rolling meadows of Marin County, California, was renovated into a sun-filled two-story cottage using architectural castoffs such as vintage mullioned French windows and doors and early-twentieth-century porcelain bath fixtures found at local flea markets. Whether it's old tin ceiling panels used to hide a modern refrigerator door, or an entire nineteenth-century apothecary recycled into a modern-day library, the homes in this book all show the creative possibilities to consider when our architectural past is recognized and appreciated.

Castoffs from another time, architectural details such as these are actually works of art on their own.

Salvage helps personalize our spaces. Often modern construction has a lack of architectural detail and warmth—touches that make a house a home—but the inclusion of vintage architecture can go a long way to remedy this. A chipped, old iron newel post reinstalled but intentionally left unpainted and unrestored, its patina now its charm after a hundred years of use; nineteenth-century encaustic tiles carefully salvaged and relaid but with all of their timeworn chips and wear left intact; an iron trivet cleverly hung as a wall sconce shade—these are the details that make the difference and help individualize a home.

Remember that everything need not be grand; even small touches can help. How about a Victorian bronze doorknob added to a modern steel door frame for an unexpected and pleasing contrast of old and new? A stained-glass window set over the kitchen sink to add its color and sparkle when the morning sun streams in? Or old school maps from the 1920s recycled and hung in the bedroom as window shades? What does make the difference is imagination, the willingness to take a risk and try something a little bit different.

Reinventing new uses for old objects is the key. Installing an oversized transom window from a nineteenth-century mansion in an otherwise nondescript, prefab bedroom addition gives the room presence and turns a small space into something special. Recycling an old wrought-iron fence into a fire screen, Victorian pocket doors into paneling for a den, even a marble-and-beveled-glass barber shop front into a master bath—with imagination, good design of any kind can be appreciated and given a new lease on life.

That's what all of the homes in this book have in common, and the secret to their successful and extraordinary interiors: imaginative uses for architectural items that most people would just pass by. Who, for example, would think to use eighteenth-century carved wooden panels from Turkey in a bedroom and combine them with bronze Tiffany wall sconces in the form of peacocks? When we visit Mrs. Ann Getty's home in San Francisco, we will see how she does this in her Turkish bedroom, getting a glimpse into her successful and creative adaptation of unusual architectural artifacts.

Another point to remember is that salvage is wonderful for children. The Novogratz family has four young children under the age of seven, all of whom love sliding down the old banisters and enjoy playing with objects that actually look better if they're a little more battered. Daily encounters with architectural salvage increases the children's appreciation of the past and helps them develop an interest in history and design from an early age.

Lost forever without the foresight and inspiration of insightful preservationists such as those featured herein, architectural salvage is our legacy, things of beauty to be proud of and to pass on to future generations. Come see how the homeowners in this book have used fragments of our architectural past to make unique and inspired interiors. Hopefully these pages will motivate more of us to consider the possibilities architectural salvage has to offer.

Turkish Treasures
on Pacific Heights

Ann Getty, wife of philanthropist Gordon Getty, has long been interested in art and architecture. Aided by the tutelage of her late father-in-law, oil billionaire J. Paul Getty, along with the occasional advice from the curators of the Getty Museum, which he founded, Mrs. Getty has gathered into her San Francisco home one of the finest collections of art and antiques in the country. The Pacific Heights mansion, built by the well-known architect Willis Polk in 1914, is a San Francisco landmark. While the sweeping views of the city and the Golden Gate Bridge are spectacular, the home's interiors are what make it special. Many of the rooms were originally decorated by well-known decorators, such as Sister Parish of the famous decorating firm of Parish-Hadley, who designed the Blue Library, but over time Mrs. Getty has added her own touches. A firm believer in the "more is better" philosophy of design, Mrs. Getty has combined layers of luxurious textiles

While the sweeping views of the city and the Golden Gate Bridge are spectacular, the home's interiors are what make it special.

Opposite: Ann Getty's Turkish bedroom is paneled in eighteenth-century Syro-Turkish painted panels and centered on an extravagant canopied bed designed after a Turkish throne. A rare Anglo Indian engraved ivory side chair is one of a pair. Exotic lighting includes a Moorish Favrile glass Tiffany table lamp at the foot of the bed and a pair of Pairpoint Puffy lamps on each side of the bed.

with museum-quality furnishings for the Georgian home in what has become her signature style, one so much admired that she opened a design firm of her own, Ann Getty and Associates, several years ago.

Mrs. Getty recognizes good design wherever she finds it, whether it's a Chinese Chippendale mantelpiece that belonged to Syrie Maugham, which she installed in her bedroom, or Rudolf Nureyev's double-sided sofa and famous patchwork drapes that now furnish her music room (Nureyev had been a guest at her home). When a large set of eighteenth-century Syro-Turkish painted panels from a Middle Eastern palace became available from an antiques dealer in Paris, Mrs. Getty did not hesitate to acquire them, even though she was not certain how they would be used. Creating successful interiors, she likes to explain, does not happen overnight, and buying objects before one has a place for them helps rooms evolve over time, much like the grand country homes of eighteenth- and nineteenth-century England.

Right: A collection of nineteenth-century Qajar painted mirrors was incorporated into the headboard.

Opposite: Fit for a harem, a corner of the room was accented with a swing made from an eighteenth-century Indian palanquin supported by cast-iron chains of animals. A Tiffany chandelier lights the swing.

Below: Intricate inlaid designs of painted wood and ivory accent the Indian swing, which is covered in nineteenth-century Central Asian textiles.

There was a sufficient quantity of the painted panels, doors and cabinet fronts to cover several rooms, and Mrs. Getty decided to install them in a guest bedroom and its adjoining dressing room in her San Francisco mansion. Even though it was eleven feet tall, the paneling did not reach the entire height of the bedroom walls, so a border of Turkish palaces complementary to the designs in the eighteenth-century panels was painted above. In the dressing room, original William Morris printed cottons were set into the wardrobe doors, their palettes of greens and Isnik blues making a surprising and quite successful juxtaposition. Using architectural artifacts in novel and unexpected ways is, in fact, one of Mrs. Getty's favorite tools of design.

The mysterious Middle East was at the height of popularity in the Western world during the last half of the nineteenth century as painters such as Eugene Delacroix depicted its sensuous and risqué pleasures. Thus, a small circa 1825–30 watercolor (originally presented to

The ornate paneling is lit by unusual nineteenth-century Tiffany bronze sconces in the form of peacocks.

Right: Closet doors in the dressing room are accented with original panels of a William Morris printed cotton whose greens and Isnik blues make a surprising and successful juxtaposition with the eighteenth-century Turkish woodwork.

Princess Charlotte, daughter of King Joseph Napoleon) by Delacroix, depicting a Turkish chieftain smoking on a divan, was an appropriate acquisition for the bedroom. As an amusing treat for the eye, the background of striped tenting in the painting was copied as a tromp l'oeil wall treatment for the hall leading into the bedroom. An ornate four-poster canopied bed based on a Turkish throne was designed, its inlaid mother-of-pearl panels and posts topped with crystal spheres and its headboard accented by nineteenth-century Qajar mirror paintings.

In a corner of the room, a late-eighteenth-century Indian painted-and-ivory palanquin (a bed used to carry nobles in processions) was made into a swing, held by figural iron chains of mythical beasts and lit by a glowing Tiffany chandelier overhead. More exotic lighting was found, including a set of six Tiffany bronze peacock wall sconces and a Moorish Favrile glass Tiffany table lamp, which was placed at the foot of the bed. A pair of rare eighteenth-century Anglo Indian engraved ivory Vizagapatam side chairs were found at auction, and other furniture pieces, including Regency painted-and-parcel-gilt page stools, were added.

The adjoining bathroom was also decorated with Turkish treasures, including a massive ten-foot-tall, cut-crystal-and-mirrored cabinet made in 1887 by the English firm of Osler in the Moghul style, and the walls were hung with Orientalist oil paintings by Gerome. The bathtub was accented with fourteenth-century inlaid mosaic panels of alabaster, red porphyry, mother-of-pearl and turquoise glass.

Now a favorite room of Mrs. Getty's guests, the Turkish bedroom exudes an air of exotic delight; one could almost expect a languid odalisque to be reclining on the palanquin swing amongst the cushions. The room has been so successful, in fact, that Mrs. Getty is now planning a second Turkish bedroom in her Hawaii home, incorporating another room of antique Turkish paneling she was fortunate enough to find. When used with imagination and style, architectural salvage can be a successful complement to even the finest interiors.

The bathtub is surrounded by fourteenth-century inlaid panels of alabaster, red porphyry, mother-of-pearl and turquoise glass.

18

The bathroom continues the
Turkish theme and is centered
on a cut-crystal-and mirrored
cabinet made in the Moghul
style by the English firm of
Osler in 1887.

19

Soho Savoy

New York City's Soho district is one of the most charming areas of the city. Streets of nineteenth-century brick-and-terra-cotta buildings are lined with smart shops and boutiques, and it is easy to believe you are in Paris or London. To find an empty lot here is unheard of, but that's exactly what Robert and Cortney Novogratz did. They bought a condemned corner building in Soho as well as the empty lot next door that was used for parking.

After restoring the three-story corner building to a single-family home, using architectural artifacts such as old theater doors and salvaged hardware and windows, they sold the building and decided to take full advantage of the 21-by-54-foot parking lot, and so drew up plans for a new townhome to be built on the site. Five stories tall with 1,200 square feet per floor, the building was designed as a single residence for just one family—the ultimate luxury in

To find an empty lot here is unheard of, but that's exactly what Robert and Cortney Novogratz did.

Opposite: An oversized ten-foot-diameter mirror from the Breakers Hotel in Palm Beach was installed in the living room, which was furnished with a comfortable sofa, floor cushions and a 1950s barber shop waiting-room chair for a lighthearted touch.

> *Robert and Cortney were both determined not to make just a "cookie-cutter" home; instead, they wanted to build something individual and unique.*

crowded, space-starved Manhattan.

Robert and Cortney were both determined not to make just a "cookie-cutter" home; instead, they wanted to build something individual and unique. Since his parents were in the antiques trade, Robert had grown up with antiques, while Cortney had been raised in a 200-year-old home in the South. Early on, both developed an appreciation of the past, as well as an innate sense of design. They began buying architectural salvage fifteen years ago while still in school, everything from doorknobs to oversized windows, knowing that they would find a use for them someday. Robert jokes that when the monthly rental fees on his storage units became more than his mortgage, he knew it was time to begin building. They began by renovating a brownstone in the Chelsea district, and then found the Soho building and accompanying lot for their next major project.

After drawing the basic floor plans (incorporating a small elevator to take the

A close-up of the newel posts shows the time-worn patina that was carefully preserved.

Right: Nineteenth-century cast-iron newel posts found in an old church were installed as eye-catching counterpoints to the stair's wooden spindles and rails.

burden out of the five flights of stairs), Robert and Cortney turned to their stash of architectural salvage for inspiration. A terra-cotta angel found in Paris became the starting point and was built into the home's exterior above the front door, setting the tone of beauty and unexpected treasure for the rest of the house. Just after giving birth to her fourth child, Cortney heard about a Victorian chapel with a beautiful encaustic tile floor being pulled down. She didn't hesitate to rush uptown to the demolition site; although the floor had already been dismantled into hundreds of individual pieces, she was not intimidated and bought the entire lot. She patiently put all of the tiles back

Between the kitchen and the living room, the open dining area is centered on a large pine farm table from Holland. Restaurant chairs, c. 1950, in their original red-vinyl upholstery are set around the table. The eighteen-foot back bar provides storage, and glass shelves were added on top for more display. An oversized stained-glass window from a cathedral lights the kitchen beyond. Note the exposed sprinkler pipes and the tin ceiling—intentionally designed to give the space a look of period construction.

Far left: Old wooden finials and a column capital on the dining table were all carefully left with their original paint intact for a more authentic look. Nickel-plated numbers from a diner are favorites with the children and adults for dinner parties.

together like a giant jigsaw puzzle for her kitchen floor.

The new townhome was carefully designed to look as if it were built in the late nineteenth century, like its neighbors. The stucco-and-brick exterior was aged with salvaged limestone columns, metallic bridge lights from the 1930s and a pair of distressed wooden doors from London, which were installed at the unassuming front entrance. Tin ceilings were used throughout the interior and the sprinkler pipes were purposefully left exposed, just as is still found in many period buildings in New York. Architectural elements were added, such as a cast-iron newel post, crusty with old paint and patina, mixed in with wooden rails as an unexpected accent on the staircase. Vintage lighting was found— metal bistro lamps from Paris, industrial, factory lamps from the forties, a trio of Victorian wrought-iron hall lamps from Georgia—and hung at different levels throughout the home to suggest age and evolution of the rooms.

*Chips and stains were left untouched on the encaustic tile floor in the kitchen to help
preserve its age and character.*

*Left: An island was built in the kitchen from the back bar and topped with a custom-
made zinc counter. Hundreds of individual encaustic tiles from a razed church were slowly
reassembled for the floor. Metal factory lights from the 1940s were hung overhead.*

On the second floor, a massive, ten-foot-diameter mullioned mirror from the Breakers Hotel in Palm Beach was installed as a focal point in the living room, its curves echoed by arched French windows opening onto the street. To keep the room from becoming too serious, Cortney added a 1950s metal-and-leather chair from a barbershop waiting room, a pile of colorful floor pillows and underneath the opulent mirror, a simple, comfortable sofa.

Another large, round, stained-glass window from a French cathedral was installed at the back of the kitchen, which was built around a kitchen island made from a nineteenth-century back bar; a striking custom-designed zinc countertop was added as machine-age contrast. The enormous, eighteen-foot-long back bar actually provided enough space for both the kitchen island and a storage cabinet across the dining area. Cortney added glass shelves to its top and filled them with favorite salvage finds—from colored seltzer bottles from the thirties and forties to nickel-plated numbers from a diner, originally used to mark an order but now equally handy for big dinner parties. Cortney couldn't resist a large hanging clock that once kept a European train station on time as a whimsical accent in the kitchen. Filled with unique architectural treasures, it's now hard to believe that this home is a mere two years old.

Even the children's rooms were designed with flair and out-of-the-ordinary architectural finds. A pair of old iron beds for the girls was dressed up with a string of pink party lights. Recycled paneled closet doors were spruced up with mirrors inset in the panels to add sparkle and shine. Distressed wooden shutters at the windows were accented with vintage fabric that, when the sunlight streams through, looks like stained glass. An old chair from a teachers' lounge in a public school was set between the beds, pupils' names still carved on the arms (Sam and Allison were among the most talented carvers). The girls chose their room's color

A pocket door in the girls' room was dressed up with brightly colored paper between panels of Plexiglas. The vanity was made from cut-down salvaged doors and Moroccan tiles.

Right: The girls chose their room color, which is dominated by bubblegum pink, and helped their mother decorate the room with architectural treasures, from old window shutters and vintage fabric on the windows to mirrors inset into the panels of a recycled closet door. The chair in the foreground is from a teachers' lounge and still has students' names carved on the arms.

scheme, which is dominated by bright bubblegum pink. For even more color, a pocket door was created from another recycled panel door, its wooden panels replaced with eye-catching panes of brightly colored paper sandwiched between Plexiglas. Cortney likes to emphasize that with her four young children (all under the age of seven) architectural antiques are a perfect choice, as the children can play in the house, slide down the banisters and decorate their rooms without fear of damaging precious furnishings—the more distressed patina the house develops, the better!

Cortney installed a large, eight-foot-tall leaded-glass window from Argentina in the master bedroom in a wall across from the stairs so that sunshine streams in from the stairwell, lit by skylights above. Her grandmother's favorite easy chair was updated with zebra-skin velvet and placed nearby, the chair's zigzag upholstery cleverly echoing the lines of the leaded-glass window.

Cortney placed some of her favorite salvage pieces in the master bedroom, including a trio of Victorian wrought-iron hall lights from Georgia, a tin cornice and carved wooden rosettes, which she hung around the window.

A roof terrace on the top of the building was completed with another terra-cotta angel set into its wall; the pair of angels are now guardians of the building from top to bottom. Robert and Cortney admit they have so enjoyed their remodels that they have embarked on yet another, even more ambitious project: restoring an entire block of four buildings, including a former NYPD station, into single-family residences. With their vision and sense of style, along with the uniqueness that only architectural artifacts can offer, we know that these buildings will be as wonderful and enchanting as their other restorations.

A large leaded-glass window from Argentina was installed in the master bedroom to allow light from the staircase into the room. Cortney reupholstered her grandmother's favorite easy chair in a striking zebra-print velvet for a distinctive and dramatic accent.

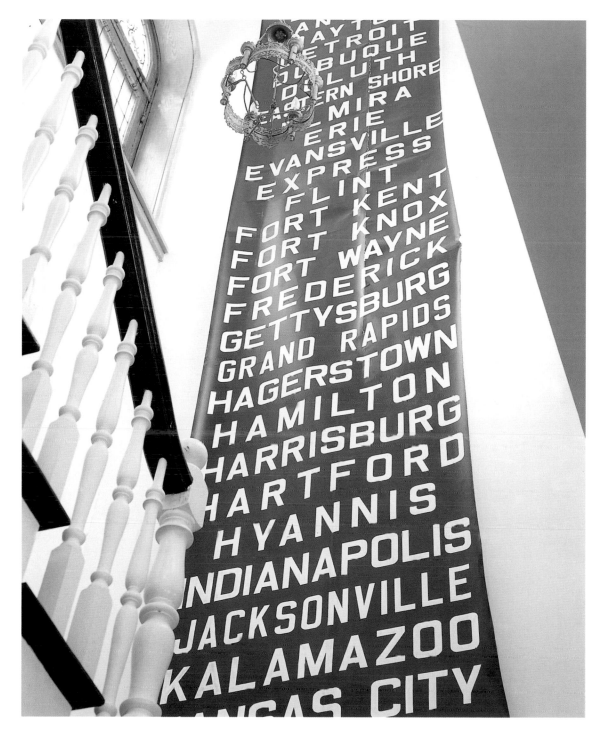

Greyhound bus station banner from the 1940s found at the flea market is the perfect accent for the tall stairwell leading to the rooftop terrace.

Left: A terra-cotta cherub's head found in Paris was set into the wall of the rooftop terrace. Flea market finds of an old green iron table and chairs make a restful spot for catching the morning sun and gazing out across the rooftops of the city.

Industrial Salvage
in Manhattan

Growing up as the son of a psychoanalyst, it's no surprise that Austin Wilke has an analytic eye. And while he became an attorney rather than an analyst, Austin nonetheless developed an appreciation early on for the subtle beauty of salvage, something he explains is like Citizen Kane's "Rosebud"—the search for his youth. Objects that reminded him of growing up in Manhattan, such as glazed metal balls that once adorned the exterior of the now-demolished Alexander's Department Store, old school maps, and a metal step stool from the New York Subway System, began to accumulate in his apartment. An older brother in the antiques trade introduced him to the flea markets in New York and he found he was drawn to industrial castoffs, old iron work, manufacturing bits and pieces—objects designed for functionality but with a beauty that most people would pass by.

Slowly his collection grew, and when he found a 1,200-square-foot

Objects that reminded him of growing up in Manhattan, such as . . . a metal step stool from the New York Subway System, began to accumulate in his apartment.

Opposite: Arts and Crafts furnishings, a 1903 Gustav Stickley table and an L. & J. G. Stickley desk and bookcase, are combined with the clean lines of industrial salvage, such as a machine shop stool and a wire wastebasket, in the 1912 apartment. Task lamps made by O. C. White at the turn of the twentieth century provide reading lights throughout the apartment.

Industrial castoffs become works of art: a brass glove stretcher, vintage wooden dice, a machinist's drill bit holder now used to hold pencils.

prewar Arts and Crafts apartment in "livable" condition in Midtown New York City, just minutes from his office as well as Central Park and his favorite jogging trails, he didn't hesitate to purchase it. The apartment was designed by brothers Edward and George Blum, early-twentieth-century architects who built apartment buildings throughout Manhattan that were noted for their handsome Arts and Crafts styling. Austin was drawn to the generous open rooms, details such as ceilings adorned with plaster strapwork, wide wooden moldings, and the large windows that let light stream in—you could almost forget you were in New York City in the late twentieth century.

Austin painted, replastered, and installed an updated galley kitchen. The "hotel apartments," built in 1912, had been designed as temporary residences for visiting Broadway performers and were not made with functional kitchens—daily maid service and bellhops would have taken care of any of the residents' needs. The major change Austin

Austin used old school maps from the 1920s and 1930s as window shades in the bedroom. Multicolored metal and ceramic balls from the 1960s, which once graced the exterior of the now-demolished Alexander's Department Store in Manhattan, hang on the wall. A rare 1934 stainless steel National Guitar Company resophonic guitar rests on the bed. The 1940s metal step stool was used to help people on and off the subways. Furniture in the room is by L. & J. G. Stickley.

37

undertook in the apartment was to remove a wall between the living and dining rooms, creating a master study/living room where he now spends most of his time.

Fascinated by its functionality of design, Austin began buying books and studying the Arts and Crafts movement. He began furnishing the apartment with Stickley pieces—an L. & J. G. Onondaga postal desk, a Gustav rocking chair, and an L. & J. G. bookcase—furniture similar to what might have been used in the apartment originally. Flea market finds and salvage store buys; simple, clean-lined industrial pieces, such as a glove maker's model of a hand; or metal, adjustable office task lamps invented by dentist O. C. White at the turn of the twentieth century, were found to complement the simple yet elegant lines of the Arts and Crafts furniture.

Austin found that salvage could be practical as well. When a former girl-friend objected to the lack of curtains at the bedroom windows, he cleverly hung

up old school maps from the 1920s and 1930s, and even found a vintage, world map light globe for the room's central light fixture, creating the ambience of an old classroom. And though the girlfriend eventually left, the maps have remained.

An iron-and-steel advertising paperweight from the late nineteenth century, simple wire wastebaskets, a machinist's wooden drill bit holder—Austin has rediscovered these and other castoffs of industrial design and elevated them to works of art. Combining these pieces with the simple, clean lines of Arts and Crafts furniture, Austin has returned his apartment to its original prewar elegance, reinterpreted as a unique and charming residence of the twenty-first century. And isn't that what makes salvage so interesting and enjoyable—finding the hidden beauty in objects that have been forgotten and discarded and successfully incorporating them in our homes today?

Flea market finds of industrial, advertising newspaper weights are used and appreciated once again.

Left: Salvage finds including a copper backsplash, Grueby tiles, an old school clock, and an iron-and-wooden stool add interest to the galley kitchen. On the cabinet, Austin composed a collage of images of the late Edie Sedgwick, a 1960s Andy Warhol superstar.

Salvage at Schooley's Mountain Springs

Schooley's Mountain Springs in rural Bergen County, New Jersey, has been known for its healing waters since the mid-nineteenth century, when people from New York City and other metropolitan areas came to "take the cure" with the spring waters and fresh mountain air believed to be beneficial for tuberculosis. Small cabins were constructed around the springs, including a one-room cottage built in 1862 on a forested slope near-by. Indoor plumbing and a small kitchen were finally added in the 1920s as the unpretentious structure began to be used year-round.

Tenants were not kind to the building, however, and by the time John Frederick and Paul Dorman looked at the 250-square-foot cabin in 1997, it was no longer habitable. It took a lot of determination to even see the property, as the real estate agent had lost the key and the only way to view it was to pry open a window and

By the time John Frederick and Paul Dorman looked at the 250-square-foot cabin in 1997, it was no longer habitable.

Opposite: Architectural salvage, such as an old window transom, is combined with flea market finds to enliven the small bedroom.

41

climb inside. There was no running water because previous thirsty tenants had removed the water tank, probably after the pipes had frozen and burst. The two rooms of the cottage—the living room and a bedroom added in the 1940s—were dark and musty. The walls were painted a dark chocolate brown and partially covered with imitation wood-grain paneling, and the floors were carpeted in a nicotine-colored shag. The bathroom had been stuccoed, its walls and ceiling painted an eye-opening mustard yellow, and the room's only window boarded up. The small kitchen, added onto a porch without foundation support, was collapsing, and it had been insulated with a creative arrangement sure to make any fire marshal pale: coffee cans filled with cooking grease and then covered over with cardboard. The kitchen walls had been used as a message board, with long-forgotten phone numbers scrawled on them from floor to ceiling. Wiring consisted of extension cords covered with silver duct tape.

Phillis, the owners' Jack Russell terrier, loves to sleep on the vintage camp blankets. Note the salvaged wooden corbel used for a shelf bracket above the bed.

Right: The small sunroom is furnished with cheerful, bright red vintage wicker covered in 1950s bark cloth.

But John and Paul were able to see through all of this and focus on the pluses. The price was affordable and the location ideal, set amongst the trees on a serene, heavily wooded hillside where there would be room for gardens and animals in a tranquil country setting. And they would be able to incorporate some of the architectural pieces they had been saving for the home's remodel. So they purchased the cottage, rolled up their sleeves, and started to work. Living without heat and hot water initially, they used a neighborhood gas station sink and bathroom; they took showers in a rental property they still possessed. After several months, the furnace was installed and the water was restored. Slowly the small house became habitable, although it took more than a year to stabilize the kitchen foundation, and meals during that time had to be cooked on a hot plate in the bathroom.

John and Paul run a successful antiques business and set up at large flea markets and antiques shows throughout

the Northeast; they would often come across unique pieces of architectural salvage. They decided to use some of them to refurbish their cottage both as a means of keeping costs down and as a way of paying tribute to salvage's often over-looked beauty and charm. Pieces ranging from old stained-glass windows and doors to vintage kitchen cabinets and appliances began to make their way into the home, and slowly its simple country charm began to reemerge.

After reinstalling the heating and plumbing and stabilizing the foundation, John and Paul turned their attention to the bathroom. Original beadboard was uncovered beneath the fiberglass shower walls and restored, and a pressed-tin ceiling was installed for a vintage look. An 1890s claw-foot bathtub was found at a flea market, and a colorful stained-glass Victorian door was recycled as a room divider between the toilet and the bathtub. John found an old oak buffet with its top missing at a yard sale and converted it into a vanity by adding a sink and

A collection of "memory ware" vases, colorful spools of thread, and old arrows add color to a corner of the den.

Right: Salvage was used throughout the bathroom, from a claw-foot tub to a Victorian stained-glass door that functions as a divider between the toilet and tub. A portrait of John's father when he was five years old hangs on the wall.

concealing the plumbing beneath for a custom look. An Arts and Crafts stained-glass window replaced the boarded up window; ceramic floor tiles were added.

The partners next tackled the narrow galley kitchen. Aiming to return the space to how it might have looked when it was first built in the 1930s, John and Paul began by laying down vintage-style green linoleum squares on the floor and painting the walls a simple creamy white. The cream-and-green color scheme was carried throughout the room—vintage cabinets were found at a tag sale, painted cream, and accented with 1930s green, glass pulls. A Depression-era porcelain sink and drain board were added, while the bottom half of an old wooden hutch was used for cabinets below the sink. A peeling green door rescued from a trash heap was installed in front of the new refrigerator to disguise the modern appliance, while a vintage green porcelain icebox was placed alongside for decorative storage. A green-and-cream porcelain gas stove from the 1920s was found at a local antiques show and restored; it now cooks well enough to serve parties of up to eighteen. A kitchen door with four wavy glass panels was salvaged from a dumpster downtown, and an old schoolhouse light fixture was put to use as overhead lighting. The kitchen now shines with the style it must have had when it was first added to the cabin seventy-five years ago.

Keeping costs down, John and Paul installed a small, 12-by-12-foot bedroom by attaching a prefabricated shed to the back of the house; the whole process took just three hours. Insulation was added and more salvage used to give the room character. An oversized, six-foot-long arched window rescued from the front door transom of a New Jersey mansion allows the dappled light of the surrounding forest to pour into the room.

The parlor is furnished with a mix of salvage and flea market finds and family pieces, from bits of Victorian stained glass to John's grandmother's oak table. John hooked the rugs himself.

Left: An 1840s Empire sofa in the parlor is paired with chairs found at flea markets and dressed up with pillows John's mother made from old quilts. Salvage finds include a painted Roaring Twenties Victrola horn hung from the ceiling.

Walls were painted a light tan pear-skin color to accent the colorful, cast-off furnishings found at tag sales and flea markets, such as a striking turquoise-blue Empire chest, and quite appropriate for the little summer cottage, a collection of vintage woolen camp blankets from the 1940s was arranged in a cheerful array of patterns and designs.

A den was added between the new bedroom and the main cabin, making use of French doors found on top of the garage when the debris was cleared away. More salvaged windows were bought at local markets for the room. Chinese red, Eisenhower-era drapes decorated with pagodas set a 1950s theme for the room, which was papered in a bright teal-and-chartreuse floral

paper of palm fronds. More 1950s accessories were found, such as a burnt bamboo rocking chair, and a collection of "memory ware," vases and pots covered with broken pottery shards in a colorful, random arrangement. A small sunroom was created off the den to take advantage of the afternoon light, and a nineteenth-century door was nailed to the wall as a sculptural work of art.

The small parlor still retained its original heart-pine floors and ten-foot ceilings that were meant to help circulate the healthy breezes. (Thomas Edison is said to have rented the cabin for a son one summer.) Salvage was used for a comfortable and eclectic country look. A mirror was made from an old window screen, and an arched, stained-glass church window was added. Flea market finds such as a Victrola horn painted with morning glories was hung from the ceiling, while a 1930s armchair was slip-covered in a period red-and-white toile. John's mother made pillows from antique patchwork quilts, and John even hooked

The narrow, galley kitchen was returned to the 1930s with cream-and-green fixtures, salvaged cabinets, and a vintage porcelain sink.

Right: Period kitchen accessories, such as a 1920s refrigerator, old tins and canisters, and cream-and-green cooking utensils add to the vintage appeal.

several rugs himself for the room. Never completely satisfied, John often rearranges the room and even repaints it during the middle of the night when he can't sleep, surprising his partner when he awakens with an entirely new decor.

Now a comfortable 750 square feet, the cabin continues to change as John and Paul make more improvements. Recent additions have included a salvaged Victorian gazebo transformed into a side porch off the kitchen and a pair of beautiful but loud peacocks, who are quite at home in their pen made from salvaged porch columns and wire mesh. It took imagination, foresight, and more than a bit of patience, but the small summer cottage has at last been restored to its picturesque rural charm.

West Village Pied-à-Terre

One of the reasons I was interested in writing this book on architectural salvage was that I knew the subject firsthand. I had restored a small, 350-square-foot pied-à-terre in New York City for my partner and myself with an array of salvaged artifacts found everywhere from the 26th Avenue weekend flea market to eBay. When we first purchased the apartment seven years ago, we liked the location in the lively West Village, and the building itself, built in the 1880s, still had its graceful brownstone exterior intact. We didn't need much room—just a small space to hang our hats when we were in town. The small tenement-style apartment seemed perfect, with just one main room, a kitchen and a small bedroom. Until the 1930s there had only been one shared water closet down the hall for each floor. Back then baths were taken in a convertible bathtub in the kitchen, which turned over to make a counter when

The small tenement-style apartment seemed perfect, with just one main room, a kitchen and a small bedroom.

Opposite: An arched Gothic door was found at the flea market to replace the vinyl accordion one on the water closet. The small bedroom was turned into a Gothic library with a hand-painted, pre-Raphaelite mural along the wall to give the room more depth. Nineteenth-century American crazy-quilt stained-glass panels were added to the window.

not in use. If you visit New York, I suggest a tour of the Lower East Side Tenement Museum, which has recreated a series of tenement apartments with this exact layout and shows how people—often up to a dozen at a time—lived in them, taking shifts sleeping in the single small bedroom.

When we first saw the apartment, it had certainly been modernized, but not significantly. While there was a private shower and water closet, the original moldings had 120 years of paint; a large built-in armoire took up half of the small living room; and the kitchen had been updated sometime in the 1960s with cheap metal cabinets and an oversized harvest gold refrigerator. The floors were covered with imitation vinyl parquet, and the glass in the transoms had been replaced with wire mesh–embedded safety glass by a previous, security-conscious resident. A plastic accordion door covered the water closet, while a large shower had been installed in a separate room whose wall extended out into the apartment, making a tight passageway past it.

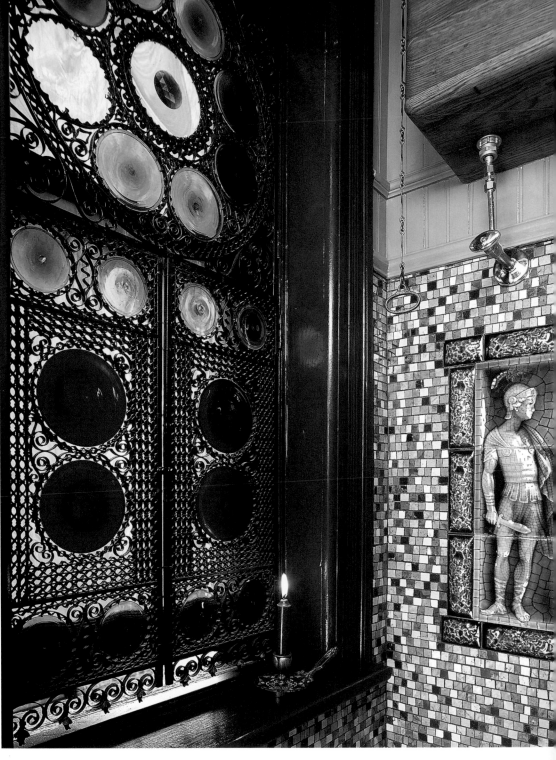

A glass-and-wrought-iron fire screen was adapted as a window screen for the water closet. Inset panels of figural American Victorian fireplace tiles dress up the hand-cut mosaic tile work on the walls.

Right: A tiny corner sink from a Victorian schoolroom was found for the shower room. The door was custom made around the painted, stained-glass window. The upper walls and ceiling are covered with hand-cut mosaic tiles, while wainscoting covers the lower sections.

The original mantel with inlaid encaustic tiles was still intact.

The shower room boasts a Victorian wall sconce in the form of a hand, a popular Victorian motif.

Fortunately, however, the simple, overall layout of the apartment had never been altered. The living room faced south onto a small, quiet courtyard. The original mantel with inlaid encaustic tiles was still intact. None of the woodwork had ever been altered, including the large interior window between the kitchen and living room, which the city had required all tenement apartments to install in

The gilded overmantel mirror has an Aesthetic movement carved sunflower. A William De Morgan vase rests on the shelf behind.

1905 to increase air circulation between the tiny, overcrowded rooms (tuberculosis was still a serious health concern). In summary, the apartment had its good bones still intact.

We began by attacking the woodwork, having it stripped in place and repainted—a very messy and time-consuming project that took nearly nine months. After having the electricity rewired and the gas replumbed (which necessitated leaving a small token of our appreciation for the gas inspector), we began, room by room, restoring the apartment to how it might

The mantel, original to the apartment, had inset encaustic tiles still intact. More antique tiles were added to the fireback, and a gilded overmantel mirror was found to just fit the space. The mantel now overflows with nineteenth-century American and English ceramics.

The parlor was going to be simple, but that resolution didn't last long. The ceiling was hand painted using a Minton tile design, and curtains that once belonged to Teddy Roosevelt were installed. Furniture includes a Kimble and Cabus Reform Gothic armchair on the right and a Hunzinger armchair recovered in a burgundy silk in the corner. The overhead chandelier, an American Aesthetic design c. 1885, features Longwy inserts and colored antique shades.

have been in the 1880s if a more affluent tenant had resided there. I frequented the flea market looking for salvage and vintage architectural pieces. I found an old brass butler's sink small enough for our limited counter space, plus a pair of faucets. We installed new cabinets in the kitchen but gave them more of a period look with Victorian brass bin pulls and vintage-style wavy glass upper fronts. I spotted a 1920s crème-and-green enameled gas stove one afternoon at the flea market, and it was a perfect fit along the narrow kitchen wall; I had it restored with both gas and electric power. An 1890s cast-iron chandelier of griffins, which had come from a nineteenth-century Boston police station, was found for the kitchen and hung from the copper ceiling we installed. A whimsical stained-glass window of a frog riding a bicycle, a stork, and other Victorian animals purchased in Portobello on a trip to London was set into the 1905 ventilation window.

More salvage was found for the water closet and shower rooms, which

Fire code required the installation of a new front door, which was enlivened with trompe l'oeuil paneling and an eye behind the Victorian cast-iron peephole cover.

Below: A Victorian stained-glass window depicting a Falconess rests on one of the parlor windows. The elaborate gold curtains, originally made for the 1893 Chicago World's Fair Japanese Pavilion and once belonging to Teddy Roosevelt, are a focal point for the room.

AND AT HER WHISTLE ON HER HAND
THE FALCON TOOK HER FAVOURITE STAND

were in different locations in the apartment. I wanted the rooms to look like subway stations (but clean) with their beautiful turn-of-the-century tiles, and so had both rooms tiled with hand-cut mosaic pieces. Antique Victorian Low Art tiles in a sunflower design were inlaid inside the shower stall, which was made narrower again, and a Victorian brass showerhead and handles were installed. I found a tiny corner sink that had come out of a Victorian schoolroom, and a vintage brass wall sconce in the form of a hand—a favorite Victorian motif (Queen Victoria was said to have thought her hands were very attractive and often had them modeled). A stained-glass panel of birds was made into a door for the shower room, with unusual square-pinned brass Eastlake hinges.

Another flea market foray turned up an arched Gothic door to replace the folding accordion door for the water closet. A high-tank toilet from the 1890s with an elephant-trunk bowl (its porcelain base curves like the trunk of an

Right: The small kitchen was completely remodeled, with new cabinets made to look old by the addition of Victorian brass bin pulls and wavy glass. The brass butler's sink came from the flea market. An English stained-glass window found at Portobello was set into the interior ventilation window between the kitchen and parlor. A copper ceiling (not visible) was installed overhead.

elephant) seemed the perfect fixture. I discovered a Victorian wrought-iron fire screen with beautiful amber roundels that just fit the opening of the bathroom window, and so had it installed as a window screen; the small room now glows during the day as light filters in through the colored-glass-and-iron screen.

A Gothic theme was carried into the bedroom, transforming it into a tiny Gothic library. A large pre-Raphaelite-inspired mural was painted along one wall to help give the small space more drama and depth, and an American crazy-quilt stained-glass window with a central panel of a painted owl was installed in the bedroom window. Bookcases in a Reform Gothic design were built for books and much-needed storage along the opposite wall.

The parlor was restored with more Victorian Aesthetic designs. We had the ceiling hand painted, based on the pattern from a nineteenth-century Minton tile, and a frieze painted around the top of the walls, emulating the inhabited

alphabet designed for the Victoria and Albert Museum's lunchrooms. I had been saving a roll of narrow, circa 1890, intricately patterned linoleum for years and found this made a perfect wainscoting for the room. Aesthetic movement furniture was found, from a Hunzinger armchair to a Kimble and Cabus Reform Gothic desk and chair. An unusual nineteenth-century radiator with an embossed stork replaced the unassuming one in the corner of the room. Vintage textiles are one of my keen interests, and I could not pass up opulent gold silk curtains with Anglo-Japanese designs that had once belonged to Teddy Roosevelt. Made for the 1893 Chicago World's Fair Japanese Pavilion, they once hung in one of his offices, and I had them reconfigured for the two parlor windows.

We were going to keep the apartment simple, just a weekend getaway, but once the process began there was no turning back. Designing with architectural salvage, I have to admit, is not only enjoyable but addictive as well.

Vermont Songwriter Salvage

It isn't always easy to find the old house of your dreams. Many need so much restoration that it isn't economical to buy them, and more often than not the location is not right. So, the next best thing often is to build your own exactly where you want it. And that's just what singer and songwriter Bobby Gosh did.

Bobby, whose songs include hits such as "A Little Bit More" and music for the Tom Hanks movie *Big*, was looking for a second home in upstate Vermont but wanted something rural and away from the madding crowd. In 1971, when he couldn't find a vintage Victorian to meet his needs, he settled instead for a small, 25-by-40-foot, recently built rambler. The house was sited in a perfect location: on six acres of rural hilltop affording sweeping views of the lush Vermont landscape. Over the next two decades, Bobby added on to the simple structure, slowly transforming it into an 8,700-square-

The house was sited in a perfect location: on six acres of rural hilltop affording sweeping views of the lush Vermont landscape.

Opposite: A nineteenth-century apothecary was dismantled and its carved golden oak shelves and cabinets made into a library for a Vermont home. Accents such as a Gothic stained-glass window, a rare Tiffany floor lamp and Art Nouveau busts add color and interest to the room. Sheet music of some of Bobby's hit songs lie on the desk.

The old apothecary shelves made perfect bookcases for Bobby's collection of antique books and paintings.

foot compound. To evoke the charm of a vintage Victorian home, he incorporated architectural salvage wherever he could, from stained-glass front doors rescued from a nearby mansion that was being turned into a nursing home, to a complete nineteenth-century New York pharmacy, which he carefully disassembled into a U-Haul, drove back to Vermont, and reinstalled as his library.

Bobby started off by adding a two-story master-bedroom-and-bath wing in 1978. While walls were still being framed, he got a phone call from a friend urging him to take a look at a barbershop being dismantled in nearby Randolph, Vermont. Built in 1919, the nearly 8-foot-tall-by-10½-foot-wide barber shop "front"—sinks, counters, drawers and mirrors—had been described in local papers as one of the finest in the state with its gleaming marble work, wide, beveled mirrors, and charming oak-and-glass cabinets.

It didn't take Bobby long to figure out how to incorporate the lucky find into his

remodel. By arranging studs in the framing to line up with the screw holes in the heavy marble panels, Bobby was able to simply mount the entire unit along one long wall, even using the original screws, which had been carefully saved during the demolition. Classic white hexagonal floor tiles visually tied the front to the rest of the bathroom, making it look like it had been built for the space. The original pair of matching pedestal sinks was included, and, luckily, all of the fittings were still intact, from the arched faucets used to wash hair to the marble drawers and small oak cabinets below for holding "sterilized" combs and scissors. Even the marble wainscoting from beneath the mirrors was reinstalled in the home. And while cowlicks are no longer cut in the old barbershop front, the beauty of its craftsmanship is still appreciated nearly a century later.

A great room was added to the back of the home to take advantage of the vistas of the surrounding Vermont countryside. Bobby added a tin ceiling and left it unsealed to better reflect the natural light back into the room. Unused 1929 Art Deco overhead fixtures were found as complements for the vintage look.

Bobby slowly acquired more than twenty acres of the verdant Vermont countryside around his house, and in 1981 decided to put a 660-square-foot kitchen, entertainment room and greenhouse addition on the back of the home to better enjoy the vista. A sloping ceiling soaring to 18 feet was designed to connect the new section to the original house.

The day before the Sheetrock was scheduled for installation, Bobby discovered a manufacturer of original 2-by-2-foot tin ceiling panels made from old factory presses that had been dormant since 1909. Inspired by the beauty of the pressed-tin panels, Bobby sent back the Sheetrock, stayed up all night, and designed and measured out precisely how many panels and in what configurations would be needed before the contractors arrived that next morning to begin work on the ceiling. A wise decision, the last-minute addition of the tin ceiling gave the room exactly the impact it needed, tying the large space together and reflecting the soft light of the surrounding valleys back into the room.

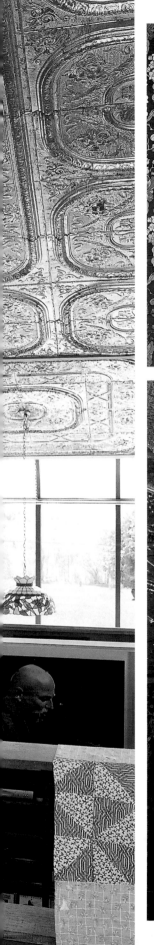

Left unsealed, the tin panels have slowly acquired a wonderful patina over the last two decades. A set of six 1929 Art Deco hanging light fixtures still in their original boxes was found at a local auction, and these were hung overhead. Four antique stained-glass windows were made into a skylight over the cooking area, and other pieces of stained glass that Bobby had collected in his travels were installed above the kitchen cabinets. A favorite spot for early morning coffee as the sun rises over the hills, the cheerful room has a Victorian charm that is rooted firmly in the twentieth century.

A collector of rare books and manuscripts, Bobby had always wanted a vintage library to properly show off his collection. And so when he got a call from antiques salvage dealer Peter Hill that

Above: One of the first windows Bobby found on the street in Brooklyn, and still one of his favorites, was installed in the kitchen.

Left; The tin ceiling and Art Deco lights add a warm glow to the great room, whose windows look out over the verdant Vermont countryside. The cranberry stained-glass window was one of many Bobby bought before he even had the house, knowing he would someday find the perfect spot for it. A greenhouse opens off the back of the great room.

the interior fittings from a nineteenth-century pharmacy in Schenectady, New York, were up for sale, he didn't hesitate. Made of golden oak, the nine-foot-tall shelves and cabinets were in remarkably good condition, and with more than forty-five linear feet, there was enough to completely cover the three walls of his current office (the fourth wall is a bank of windows). Bobby hired a crew, carefully dismantled the old apothecary, and brought it back to Vermont. He then contacted cabinetmaker and architectural woodworker Peter Maynard to retrofit the woodwork into a library. Setting up a makeshift shop in Bobby's garage, Maynard was able to take the disassembled sections of shelves and cabinets and, after careful measuring, install them so precisely that they looked like they had been made for the space. Because the shelves were solidly built, Maynard was able to use the preexisting nailing battens under the counters and at the tops of the bookcases to simply screw the units into the wall studs. Corners

Right: Bobby found an entire 1919 barbershop front, including the sinks, cabinets, mirrors and marble wainscoting and countertops, and used it to create a stunning master bath.

Above: Even the original oak-and-glass "sterilizer" cabinets were still intact in the barbershop and now make perfect bathroom storage.

were carefully mitered with a hand-saw and strips of egg-and-dart crown molding applied where they were missing. The wood was finished with a high tung-oil varnish for a luster that highlighted the beautiful golden oak perfectly. Bobby already had other architectural accents in the room, including a magnificent 1848 stained-glass window from a local church and pocket doors complete with their Eastlake hardware from a nineteenth-century mansion. Lit with the warm glow of Tiffany lamps, the old apothecary shelves have been given a second life as a warm and inviting library.

And that's what architectural salvage is all about—saving and reusing bits and pieces of old buildings and construction, reminders of the talent and artistry of the past, and in the process preserving them for future generations to enjoy.

Midtown Manhattan

Makeover

Midtown Manhattan is a bustling place. Skyscrapers and high-rises tower along every block, and the stream of people and honking horns is constant—hardly the spot, you would think, for a quiet Arts and Crafts apartment building from the turn of the twentieth century to survive. But when George and Edward Blum built the twenty-story Adlon "hotel apartment" in 1912 off Broadway, it made perfect sense. In the heart of the Theater District, the building soon became a favorite residence for actors and entertainers of the day, from Bela Lugosi and Art Carney to Whitey Ford. Apartments were built in the newly fashionable Arts and Crafts style, with handsome woodwork and moldings, large mullioned windows, even oak-and-tile fireplaces in the front parlors. Meant for the well-heeled Manhattanite, amenities included bellhops, daily maid service, and even tiny built-in wall safes in the master bedrooms for safeguarding the wife's

Apartments were built in the newly fashionable Arts and Crafts style, with handsome woodwork and moldings, large mullioned windows, even oak-and-tile fireplaces in the front parlors.

Opposite: Michael Laudati's parlor features the original plaster strapwork ceilings and generous windows. Michael has furnished it with an Arts and Crafts settle and chairs, all found at local flea markets. The mantel was found at a salvage store, as was the overhead brass chandelier with Favrile glass shades. Wall sconces were original to the apartment.

71

pearls and diamonds after a night out on Broadway.

Well-built, the building remained apartments for the next seventy years until it was converted into co-ops. The lobby was then "updated" and much of its character removed, a fate many of the apartments also suffered over time. When Michael Laudati and his wife, Despina, first saw their apartment, it was in "estate" condition, actually two apartments sold as one 1,700-square-foot unit. The woodwork had been painted mint green throughout, and the inlaid parquet floors were covered with brown shag carpeting. The kitchen—never meant to be large, as these apartments were not considered permanent homes—had no cabinets, and the single long counter was covered in orange Formica. Even the imitation brick walls in the kitchen had been painted over in mint green. But after one three-minute viewing, Michael and Despina were hooked. The original wide six-over-one windows had never been replaced, and their unusual side casement panels let in a

An Arts and Crafts hall lantern with its original opalescent glass shade was hung in the foyer.

Far right: Michael stripped and restored the golden oak mantel that he found at a local salvage store and added mosaic tiles around the inside.

Below: An old mirrored closet door, pieces of trim, and vintage coat hooks were used to make a built-in hall tree.

An Arts and Crafts hand-hammered brass chandelier with an unusual glass shade was found at a local salvage store to light the hallway.

Below: Michael installed an Arts and Crafts hammered-brass chandelier in the entryway of the building.

The dining room, originally a combination living room and dining room, was restored by replacing the "updated" aluminum windows with six-over-one mullioned windows that matched those in the rest of the apartment. Original wainscoting was refinished and a plate rail restored on top. While working on a movie in Chicago, Michael found another Arts and Crafts pan light at a local antiques shop and added it above the dining room table.

More salvage was found for the bathroom. Michael came across an 1890s marble sink top at a flea market, which he fashioned into a pedestal sink by adding old moldings to the sides and wooden table legs for the feet. A medicine cabinet was made from a cache of old trim work and two panels of stained glass were found at a salvage shop, where he also found an early-twentieth-century claw-foot tub. The room's original seven-foot-tall subway tiles were fortunately still intact, and Michael accented these with a floor of marble tiles offset with glass-mosaic squares in the corners, an homage to the Blums' Arts and Crafts

Michael found an oak Arts and Crafts mantel and installed it in the lobby to create a focal point for a seating area.

aesthetic. The 1930s toilet was left in place. A simple Edison light with a milk glass shade, found at another salvage yard, lends a warm glow to the room.

While Michael worked on his apartment, it wasn't long before he turned his eye to the building's double lobbies, which had been heartlessly "sanitized" in the 1980s. Michael was able to return the lobbies to their original Arts and Crafts elegance by recasting Celtic-patterned custom moldings, replicating light fixtures and entrance doors from period photographs, and even discovering original 1912 Grueby floor tiles still intact underneath the modern white-ceramic replacement

Michael used old sections of wrought-iron fencing to make a headboard and footboard for his bed. His miniature greyhound loves to sleep on the bed. Notice the original small wall safe to the right of the window; it was installed when the building was first built as an "apartment hotel" for visiting Broadway performers.

Left: The handsome original strapwork ceiling in the dining room was still intact. Michael restored the plate rail and found a period brass chandelier to hang above the dining room table.

The bathroom sink and cabinet were made from a salvaged sink top, stained-glass panels and wooden table legs. The claw-foot tub was also found at a salvage shop. The wall tiles are original.

tile floor. Michael used salvage in the lobby restoration in creative ways, such as recycling old doorplates and brass shelf brackets to make period-looking wall sconces, and installing old brass mail slots as recessed lighting for the entrance steps.

Word of Michael's skills soon spread, and he was awarded the Victorian Society's prestigious Best Grassroots Preservation Award of 2003 for the Adlon lobby restoration. Rejuvenation of a building is not all that different from creating makeup, Michael explains, as both are ways of restoring beauty, whether it's to a person's face or the entrance of a building. Michael's skills are in such demand that he has launched a second career, still as a cosmetologist but now for buildings in need of a little makeover. With his expert craftsmanship and handiwork, along with well-chosen pieces of salvage, Michael works his movie-like magic, bringing back the beauty and grace of the Arts and Crafts era to lucky residents of George and Edward Blum's buildings.

San Francisco Splendor

San Francisco has one of the finest and largest collections of Victorian homes in the country. Turreted and gingerbread-encrusted row houses line the hilly streets throughout the city, and many have been restored to their nineteenth-century splendor, often with the assistance of salvaged architectural details. One such restoration on the steep crest of a hillside above the city has been the work of Keith Adams. Attracted by the panoramic views of downtown San Francisco, Keith and his partner, Jeff Madeiros, fell in love with the 1897 Victorian, even though it had been divided into five rental units and much of its original detailing was gone. They were well used to home restorations, this project being the third they had undertaken in San Francisco in the past eight years.

Keith in particular has always had a love of old homes and architecture. Born and raised in the South, Keith was

Attracted by the panoramic views of downtown San Francisco, they fell in love with the 1897 Victorian, even though it had been divided into five rental units.

Opposite: The front parlor was dressed up with mirrored paneling from the French Consulate in Tanzania. A Victorian marble mantel was also added. The antique furniture includes a pair of nineteenth-century French fauteuils, an 1857 Viennese piano and an 1820 tea safe from Virginia. The Art Deco chandelier makes a striking accent to the formal antique furnishings.

nurtured on a long family tradition of preservation, and country homes and plantations have been a part of his family's heritage since the 1690s. Keith recalls collecting old millstones from family plantations as a child, and by the time he was in college he had begun salvage hunting in earnest, dismantling an 1840s plantation slated for demolition and recycling it for a home in Arkansas. By the time he began restoration of this Victorian in San Francisco, Keith admits, the salvage bug had become a serious affliction. He had searched out salvage across the country, as well as in England and France, and even had his own warehouse to store his ever-accumulating treasures. A set of mirrored doors from the French

Keith approached the restoration of the San Francisco home wisely . . .

Paneling in the den is made from old pocket doors and recycled molding from a church. The painting above the sofa was commissioned by the Duke of Wellington to celebrate his defeat of the French at Waterloo.

Left: The mirrored doors were built out from the wall to create a narrow storage area for paintings and picture frames.

Top left: Rescued from a demolished cafe, the chandelier was so large that no one else was interested in it. Here it is the perfect counterpoint to the room's more formal furnishings.

Consulate in Tanzania, hardware from a Victorian mansion in Toronto, and a huge Art Deco chandelier no one wanted because of its size were all carefully saved for future reuse.

Keith approached the restoration of the San Francisco home wisely, keeping an overall plan in mind to avoid a mixture of architectural styles that would become confusing. Treating each architectural piece as its own work of art, he tied the diverse elements together with color and form. Massive, eight-foot-tall painted mirror panels from a demolished San Francisco Roaring Twenties dinner club were chosen as a starting point. Keith had come across the entire set of more than thirty pieces of painted glass, which had been stored in a basement for thirty years, when the workman who had originally rescued the windows from the landfill decided to sell them. Keith methodically drew paper silhouettes of each window and pinned them to the walls, carefully aligning them to balance proportionately in the stairwell and upper hallway.

Oversized moldings were designed to frame each window and make it stand alone as a work of art. Keith painted the areas behind the windows ochre to highlight each window's color and reflection, but carefully avoided restoring or repairing defects so as to retain their original character and charm.

The hallway walls were painted a soft gray-blue to subtly tie the large pieces together. Keith was able to incorporate nine of the windows in the hall and two more in an upstairs bath. Originally a small fainting room, the space was converted into a bathroom with two gold-leafed, painted, mirrored panels set between a nineteenth-century gold-leaf mirror and a strikingly modern glass sink. Iron railing from a downtown San Francisco building became the perfect banister and rails, while a massive 1870s rusting cast-iron building front with its original paint and gold stenciling still intact, rescued in a small California town, was recycled as a handsome door frame for the master bedroom.

Heads of phoenixes adorn the handles of the early-nineteenth-century bronze hardware on the hall bookcases.

Left: Originally bought for kitchen cabinets, the tall windows from a razed Victorian in Oakland made perfect hallway bookcases, Keith decided, with their crusty patina carefully kept intact. The crystal chandelier, c. 1850, came from a mansion in Savannah. The tall case clock is Belgian c. 1900. A French pine-and-wrought-iron door in the back hall leads to a rear bedroom.

One of the home's most attractive features was the sweeping view of downtown San Francisco from the second floor. Keith, in fact, has period photographs of the home following the 1906 San Francisco earthquake and subsequent fire, showing his Victorian standing proud on the peak of the hill while San Francisco below was engulfed in flames. Three small rooms at the back of the home were combined into a large living-dining space to take advantage of the view. A jumble of circa-1850s redwood columns and pilasters found at a salvage yard for $75 were pieced back together and used to frame the space, while nineteenth-century wall panels and mirrors from the Tanzanian French Consulate filled the spaces in between. A Victorian marble mantel was installed as a focal point and a vintage 1940s iron-and-crystal chandelier hung above the dining table. Furnishings from modern Barcelona chairs to an 1820s Empire mahogany dining table (found covered in mud at a yard sale) were combined to

A Victorian cast-iron fence was used as the upstairs hall railing. Keith found the massive cast-iron storefront in an alley and recycled it as a door frame to the master bedroom. He carefully kept all of the original paint and patina untouched.

Top right: Keith found the fence railing in a local salvage yard and reused it as the staircase railing. Opulent painted panels on mirrors from the 1920s were installed in the stairway and upper hall.

Right: Gilded Art Deco mirrored panels coordinate beautifully with a vintage Victorian mirror in the upstairs bath.

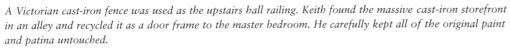

86

A striking bathroom was created out of a small upstairs fainting room by contrasting Art Deco painted mirror panels and a gilded Victorian mirror with modern features such as a sleek glass sink, white marble floors and glass blocks around the shower.

make the room stylish, sophisticated and still very personal. Keith wanted deep, vintage-style cabinets in the kitchen off the dining room; so he found old windows with their wavy glass fronts still intact and had generous cabinet boxes built behind them. Old slabs of marble were recycled for the countertops, and an 1840s jeweled Indian light fixture was hung above the sink for an exotic touch.

A set of early-nineteenth-century paneled and mirrored doors from the French Consulate in Tanzania (found on a trip to Paris) were used to panel the downstairs parlor; they were set out fourteen inches from the wall to create a hidden and handy storage area for paintings and frames. An oversized, six-foot Art Deco chandelier from a local cafe being demolished was installed as a striking counterpoint to the formal paneling. Woodwork was painted a mossy gray-green to

Detail of the mirrored paneling.

harmonize with and tie the room's features together. (Keith had it painted six times before he was satisfied with the color.)

Keith continued his use of salvage in the den, where he recycled Victorian pocket doors into paneling for the walls, framed by molding from an old church. Salvaged French glass doors

and ornate Victorian hardware from Toronto finished off the space. And one of Keith's favorite finds —a set of crusty tall windows from a demolished Victorian mansion in Oakland—were converted into a built-in glass-fronted bookcase in the hall, accented with French bronze hardware featuring handles with the heads of phoenixes.

Now that this restoration has been completed, Keith has already begun his next: a large high-rise condominium with sweeping vistas of the city. Initially promising to keep the project simple, Keith admits he already has had thoughts of using the rest of those mirrored glass panels on one wall and maybe accenting another with vintage Zuber wallpaper. Keith concedes he is addicted to salvage—not such a bad vice, most would agree.

The dining area upstairs is framed by redwood columns that were found in a large pile and methodically pieced back together. Keith found the Empire mahogany dining table at a yard sale, covered in mud.

Left: The upper kitchen cabinets were made from salvaged windows with their wavy glass still intact, and the counters were built from recycled marble.

NYC Warehouse Restoration

When Carter Smith was looking for a building to restore in New York City, he knew what he wanted: something with character, a bit out of the ordinary, and with enough room to incorporate his growing collection of artifacts—everything from the pair of elk antlers his parents had given him for Christmas to the de-accessioned massive bathtub once used by the head mistress of a Victorian girls' school. When he told his real estate agent his requirements and his budget, his agent simply laughed, and then admitted there was one derelict warehouse near Seaport that had been on the market for a long time but had not had any buyers because of its deplorable condition.

Condemned for demolition by city inspectors, the narrow (18½-foot-wide) four-story brick warehouse had been built in 1824 on a ship chandler's canal; boats docked at its front door and cargo was loaded through the front windows. The canal was eventually filled in as the

When he told his real estate agent his requirements and his budget, his agent simply laughed.

Opposite: An antique soapstone double sink was installed in the second-floor kitchen. The original brick walls were left exposed to add to the industrial look of the warehouse, while 175-year-old ceiling beams were found to replace the badly damaged originals. Antique French cafe lights with silvered-glass shades add sparkle to the room. Spindles on the stairs came from the servants' staircase at Royal Albert Hall in London. Notice the wide floorboards from an 1870s dairy barn.

The open shelf was made from a floor plank from the dairy barn and supported by brackets and hooks from a French butcher shop. Glass jars from an apothecary and taxidermy ducklings add a lighthearted touch.

city grew, and the building was made into apartments with a shop on the ground floor. A previous owner had stripped the interior several decades ago, intending to make the warehouse into a single-family home, but had abandoned the project. By the time the agent showed it in 2001, a fire had gutted most of the remaining interior; there were gaping holes in the floors; the staircase was unusable; and birds were nesting inside. In fact, the old brick structure was so weak that it would have already collapsed had it not been supported by adjacent buildings.

But the homeowner fell in love with the abandoned warehouse the moment he walked inside. The 175-year-old brick walls were still intact, and the south-facing building admitted soft, beautiful light. The quiet little neighborhood, tucked between Wall Street and the waterfront, was a hidden oasis from the hectic pace of surrounding Manhattan, the perfect place to begin arranging his accumulating treasures. So Carter purchased the building and began its restoration with the help of architect Jim Joseph.

Below: The opposite side of the kitchen is centered on a French La Cornue range, with an open shelf made from an old floorboard. The cabinets and soapstone counters are new. The large table was made in India in the late 1880s for British export. Vintage lighting includes an overhead fixture from an old factory, as well as French cafe lights.

Top: Antique hardware pulls were added to the kitchen cabinets, including this unusual c. 1875 example decorated with the head of a dog.

The open shelf was made from a floor plank from the dairy barn and supported by brackets and hooks from a French butcher shop. Glass jars from an apothecary and taxidermy ducklings add a lighthearted touch

Carter Smith, a fashion photographer, has a trained eye for layout and design. He travels the world on fashion shoots, from Paris to Rome to Rio de Janeiro, and is constantly visiting new and beautiful interiors. As soon as he saw the gutted interior of his acquisition, he knew exactly what he wanted to do. In the tradition of

95

Old and new are creatively combined in the third-floor living room and study. Weathered 175-year-old ceiling beams and exposed brick walls are softened by simple green velvet drapes. The ebonized bookcase was built in and accented by a vintage wall sconce with crystal shade and old mirrors behind the shelves. The furniture is a mix of a comfortable leather Chesterfield sofa found in Ireland, a pair of Victorian tufted chairs reupholstered in white muslin, and a pink vinyl Moroccan ottoman from the 1950s. A moose antler rests on the windowsill.

the building's shop-front history, he would keep his office and workspace on the ground floor, then create a series of living quarters above that, linking all floors with a curving steel staircase.

The original wooden ceiling beams had been so badly damaged by the fire that they were not salvageable, and so similar beams from an 1830s mill were located. Each beam was hand planed before installation to fit the existing brick pockets in the walls.

The biggest restoration challenge was the floor. While vintage flooring was called for in the restoration, such a large amount was needed that it seemed an impossible task. Then one morning Carter's architect told him about a nineteenth-century dairy barn being dismantled in Upstate New York. He promptly cancelled all of his appointments, drove to the site, and purchased the entire lot as it was being off-loaded from the truck. The old planks varied in size and had a wonderful patina that can only come with age. He simply scrubbed them with a wire brush,

hosed them down, and installed them unsealed so their mottled and stained character would continue to shine through.

Many areas of the original brick walls required patching with newer bricks, but rather than disguising the additions, it was decided to leave the new areas untouched; the exposed bricks then became a map of the building's restoration. Roof tiles were found, and street pavers salvaged from ancient flooded cities in China's Yangtze Valley were put in place on the roof to create a lovely garden terrace.

Once the building's foundation and framework had been restored, a living area was designed for each floor. The second floor became the kitchen and dining area. An old soapstone double sink was found in Maine and installed along with vintage faucet handles plus a clever touch—brass-plated hospital-operating-room foot pedals beneath the sink to turn on the water. New vintage-style cabinets were built and soapstone counters added; both are expected to age well. Other special finds included stairway spindles from

the servants' stairs at Royal Albert Hall in London, wrought-iron shelf brackets and a butcher's rack of hooks from Paris, and vintage hanging lamps with silvered shades from a French cafe. A rare British export table made in the 1880s in India was found for the dining table, and whimsical touches, such as taxidermy ducklings and Victorian apothecary jars, were added.

A living room and study on the third floor was built around custom-designed, ebonized wall cabinets inset with antique mirrored backs and lit by sconces with vintage crystal shades. Comfortable furniture, including a leather English Chesterfield sofa, tufted Victorian chairs covered in muslin, and a pink vinyl ottoman from the fifties, along with art such as a friend's Plexiglas box of shattered exit signs, are all highlighted against the ancient ceiling beams and rough, exposed brick walls.

The bathroom on the fourth floor was built around one of the more unusual salvage finds—a large, freestanding Victorian porcelain tub that once belonged

An apothecary cabinet was turned into the master bath vanity, centered with a vintage sink and accented by simple, industrial-style lighting. The green metal chair is from the 1950s.

to the headmistress of a prestigious nineteenth-century girls' school. A pair of elk antlers, a gift from the homeowner's parents, made a perfect towel rack, while a worn and distressed chopping block proved useful as a bathing table beside the tub. An apothecary cabinet across the room was installed as a vanity and inset with a vintage sink found in Maine.

The fifth floor became the master bedroom, accommodating such salvage as a desk made from the extra floor planks.

Carter Smith likens his warehouse to a giant jigsaw puzzle, the addition of diverse architectural salvage being the key to transforming it into a cohesive whole. With his sense of design and creativity, he has successfully turned a once-condemned warehouse into his personal vision of an extraordinary home.

The homeowner had always wanted a bathtub he could walk completely around, and thus he could not resist this porcelain Victorian example that had once belonged to the headmistress of a girls' boarding school. The elk antlers were a gift from his parents. A French wooden chopping block found in Los Angeles makes a pleasing complement to the rough brick walls and wooden ceiling beams. Vintage factory lights add to the industrial look.

Thirties Glamour
in Greenwich Village

Glamour is finally back. Opulent rooms accented with silvered and mirrored furniture, glittering chandeliers and luxurious furs are replacing sparse, minimal interiors. A throwback to the 1930s when opulence was in, homeowners are rediscovering the joys of feathering their nests with the style and drama of the silver screen, when sirens such as Mae West and Gloria Swanson swept through lavish interiors of crystal chandeliers and chaises piled high with fur pillows and throws.

Mark Fields and Greg Ventra, owners of Venfield Antiques in New York's Greenwich Village, specialize in glitter and glam; their shop is filled with mirrored tables and chests from the 1930s and 1940s, crystal and silver cigarette boxes and lamps, and fabulous (real and fake) fur pillows and throws.

When they decided to open their shop in 2002, the partners wanted to find a building they could live in as well, and

A throwback to the 1930s when opulence was in, homeowners are rediscovering the joys of feathering their nests with the style and drama of the silver screen . . .

Opposite: A simple nineteenth-century mantelpiece was added to the master bedroom. Walls were painted a soft gray and glamorous furnishings were added, including the pair of mirrored chests and black suede ottoman from the 1940s.

101

An oak mantel found in Harlem was installed in the guest bedroom and dressed up with a collection of Staffordshire dogs.

they weren't afraid of a little work. They had just finished restoring a nineteenth-century townhouse uptown and had the energy for another project. So when they found the brownstone on Bleeker Street in the West Village, they didn't hesitate to make an offer. Built in 1859 by William Snodgrass, a local contractor, the building was a modest four-story structure designed to house the servants of wealthy neighbors who lived in grander townhomes around the corner. Since many of the buildings on Bleeker already had stores on the ground floor, Snodgrass had included a shop front on his as well, accented with a large window edged in handsome copper trim. The building remained a shop with apartments above for the next century, and by the 1920s a beauty salon occupied the ground floor.

Time and tenants were not very kind to the building, however, and by the time Mark and Greg found it listed for sale, maintenance had been deferred for decades and the entire building had significant damage and deterioration. Rooms

Hardware from the 1920s was kept for the period look and dressed up with silver-plated back plates.

were filled with garbage and the floors were so rotten that one could see all the way through from the ground to the fourth floor. The original mahogany staircase had been replaced sometime in the 1970s with industrial metal stairs, fireplaces were removed in the apartments, and much of the original trim and woodwork had disappeared. But Mark and Greg were not put off and saw the building as a perfect fit for their needs. So the partners bought the building and began the extensive renovation.

Since their store specialized in antiques from the glamorous years of the 1930s, Mark and Greg decided to return the building to such opulence as well, decorating it as if the patrons from the beauty salon had lived upstairs. Historic Review Board standards for the exterior restoration were based upon 1920s specifications, and these helped guide their decisions. Six-over-six windows were built to replace modern sashes. Floors were rebuilt and molding and trim were added where they had been missing (raised panels under the windows were fortunately still intact). A major part of the remodel was replacement of the metal staircase. Antique spindles were found at a salvage yard and a mahogany handrail was replicated to match the gracefully curved original. Vintage fireplaces, found everywhere from demolitions in Harlem to New York salvage yards, were added. The original nineteenth-century hardware had been updated in the 1920s with glass doorknobs and escutcheons, and these were retained to keep with the Art Deco design; the escutcheons were silver-plated for an extra touch of class.

The master bedroom became an ode to Moderne, centered on a pair of 1940s mirrored chests of drawers. A 1940s black suede ottoman with nickel-plated studs, a bold-striped zebra skin underneath and a nickel-plated alabaster pan light overhead helped complete the elegant, sophisticated look. The guest bedroom was centered on a simple mantel found in Harlem, dressed up with a whimsical collection of Staffordshire

Left: A life-sized 1920s marble horse head from China greets visitors to the apartment and sets the tone of glamour and high style. Mirrored furniture from the 1940s adds to the look.

Below: An ornate mantel from a Gramercy Park mansion was added as a focal point for the living room. Fur pillows and throws and a chair covered in zebra skin add to the lush and exotic look.

dogs. A 1910 amethyst-and-rock-crystal chandelier from France was added to fill the room with a sparkling glow.

Glamour was introduced to the living room as well. Walls were painted a rich charcoal gray, and the room centered on an elaborate 1870s mantel, originally from a Gramercy Park mansion and found at a local salvage shop. More mirrored furniture, such as an Italian coffee table from the 1940s, was added and accented with luxurious animal skins, including an 1840s leopard skin found in Paris, as well as new mink and chinchilla pillows and throws that Mark and Greg carry in their shop. A nineteenth-century Portuguese chair was recovered with a zebra skin (including the tail) to add to the exotic appeal. The partners placed a massive, 750-pound marble horse head that originally came from the Belgian Embassy in China in the foyer. Made in the 1920s, it is the perfect accent, setting the tone of opulence and elegance for the home. Make no mistake, when combined with the right architectural salvage, glamour makes a winning décor.

Marin County Magic

Marin County, California, is a magical place. Above San Francisco, just north of the Golden Gate Bridge, Marin County has been the home of picturesque communities set amongst the towering redwood forests since the 1850s, and many towns still retain their old-fashioned quaintness and charm. This is exactly what attracted Derek Webb to the tiny hamlet of Ross, which he discovered while on a mountain-bike ride one afternoon in 1998. Founded as a resort town in the 1860s for wealthy San Franciscans, its houses were originally built along long, narrow lots following the line of the railroad that brought the city dwellers first to Tiburon and then farther north to the unspoiled countryside of Ross. A simple Dutch Colonial built in 1902 along with its turn-of-the-twentieth-century gabled barn next door was for sale that afternoon when Derek rode by.

But it was the barn, not the house, that made him stop in his tracks. That's

A simple Dutch Colonial built in 1902 along with its turn-of-the-twentieth-century gabled barn next door was for sale that afternoon when Derek rode by.

Opposite: A great room was created on the main floor of the barn, which overlooks a flagstone patio and pool. Arched, mullioned windows from France were combined with French doors found in Oakland to create a light and airy retreat. Hand-hewn beams from an Amish barn, c. 1800, were used for the walls and ceiling, for a rustic carriage-house look, while an antique chandelier from France provides an elegant note.

A French stonemason created the massive fireplace from local Sonoma fieldstone as a focal point of the room. The television is cleverly concealed behind weathered window shutters. A mixture of casual furniture and antiques found at local flea markets fills the room.

because Derek had always wanted to live in a barn. Born and raised in New England, he had been fascinated early on with old houses and salvage. His grandfather had restored a rambling Victorian mansion in Larchmont, New York, and Derek used to enjoy helping him. In high school he collected and traded early New England antiques, tools, sleighs, and bottles and recalls paneling his entire dorm room at Deerfield Academy in vintage barn wood (he saved the paneling and used it again for his college room at Dartmouth, as well). Following very successful careers on Wall Street and then as a global money manager, Derek found himself living in San Francisco and looking for the right home, something unique, where he could indulge his passion for architectural artifacts and antiques. A barn in Ross was the perfect solution.

Time, however, had not treated the barn kindly. Following a fire in the 1970s, the barn had been rebuilt with aluminum siding and sliding glass windows and made into a duplex. A drug dealer and a

A Victorian sad iron and a plaster corbel hold a collection of vintage books on the mantelshelf, which is made from a hand-hewn beam from a c. 1800 Amish barn. The Sonoma fieldstone mantel was all laid without mortar by a French stonemason, who spent more than three years working on projects around the property.

A collection of varying oak newel posts found in Vermont, along with railings from Stamford, Connecticut, were used for the stairs. Vintage oak treads were found in France, and a brass foot railing for a bar was recycled as the banister along the wall.

practicing witch—neither of whom were fastidious housekeepers—had been the most recent occupants. So Derek decided to start completely over, tearing down the barn to the studs but remaining within the original envelope of the building. As he traveled the globe on business, he would sneak away whenever he could, whether in Hong Kong, Paris or New York, searching out salvage yards and looking for architectural elements for his barn.

And so nine sets of matching nineteenth-century arched-and-glazed French doors were discovered stashed in the third subbasement of a Manhattan tenement; these Derek combined with matching arched glazed doors from an Oakland salvage yard to frame the main floor of the barn. Aiming for the look of a nineteenth-century carriage barn, he used distressed circa-1800 hand-hewn beams taken from an Amish barn in Pennsylvania as exposed timbering on the walls and ceilings. Derek still has fond memories from his childhood of beautiful drywall stonework on the houses and fences in Connecticut,

A hand-hammered wrought-iron chandelier, c. 1910, from a Bordeaux winery hangs in the center of the upstairs home office.

Left: The second floor is a light-filled home office, fitted with large French windows found in France that open out over the pool and gardens. The floor was made from old barn flooring. A collection of Derek's favorite architectural finds includes a European railroad clock hung over the desk and Australian gumwood cabinets (not shown) lining the opposite wall of the room.

where he was raised, and when he was introduced to a gifted French stonemason who could build exquisite dry-stack stone walls like those he grew up with, he didn't hesitate to hire him. Derek had a commanding dry-stack fireplace of local Sonoma fieldstone built as the focal point of the main room of the barn and was so impressed with the work that he had the mason construct dry stack walls around the entire perimeter of the property, a project that took more than three years.

A staircase leading to the second story of the barn was built from vintage oak stair treads found in France, newel posts from Vermont, and wood railings from Stamford, Connecticut. Upstairs, two bedrooms and a bath were added, using, of course, salvaged treasures that included barn-wood floors, a shower from New York's Knickerbocker Hotel, and a vintage sink and toilet found at local flea markets. Derek designed a bright and airy home office on the second floor, constructed around a large set of 1880 Australian gumwood library cabinets. Victorian

Vintage furnishings in the guest bedroom include a 1920s jadeite-green painted dresser and bed, c. 1900 oak chairs with their original yellow and blue coats of paint still intact, and a 1920s rusty green advertising tin can.

Eastlake doors, salvaged hardware (Derek bought a garbage can filled with hardware odds and ends on a trip to New Orleans and was able to reconstruct and use most of it) and lighting such as a hand-hammered iron chandelier from a Bordeaux winery added to the rustic look.

Once the barn was finished, Derek landscaped the surrounding grounds, adding a flagstone terrace and swimming pool between the barn and the house, where salvage was used liberally.

As an investment expert, Derek firmly believes that architectural salvage is an excellent investment; a limited commodity, it will only appreciate with time. As the world shrinks, becoming more uniform and standardized, the more unusual will become the more valuable; e.g., a handmade door will retain its economic as well as aesthetic value much longer than the prefabricated alternative. Derek's rustic barn in rural Marin County is not only a beautiful restoration but also makes good economic sense, too.

Nineteenth-century cupboard doors with their distressed, buttery yellow paint carefully left intact were recycled into closet doors in the guest bedroom. The wall next to the cupboard is paneled in old barn-wood siding. More flea market finds include a birdhouse and an old advertising sign. A Victorian child's Windsor chair rests in the corner.

Left: The second guest bedroom is also dressed in salvaged barn siding. Furnishings such as the mirror have their patina and old paint purposely left untouched, for a rustic look. The lamp was made from the mast of a racing ship the owner's father crewed in the America's Cup.

Birmingham Basics

Roy Morton was raised in Birmingham, Alabama, and always had an interest in antiques. His mother was an antiques dealer, and as a young man he began buying and selling period salvage from the garage behind his mother's home. Old doors, windows, mantels, and garden ornaments soon began overflowing his makeshift shop, and as word spread, Roy found he was developing a full-time business. He moved to larger quarters in downtown Birmingham in 1995 and began importing architectural elements from Europe, going on buying trips to England and France several times a year. Massive stone fireplaces from Normandy chateaux, heavily carved doors from English manor houses, and statuesque terra-cotta chimney pots from the roofs of English lodges began to crowd his shop.

Roy had met his wife, Becky, in college and one of their favorite activities was to go antiquing on the weekends.

Old doors, windows, mantels, and garden ornaments soon began overflowing his makeshift shop, and as word spread, Roy found he was developing a full-time business.

Opposite: The cottage's parlor is decorated with a mix of comfortable furniture and favorite salvage. The English oak fireplace was added to replace the original, which had been removed by previous owners. Roy's grandfather's traveling valise now doubles as a side table. A Georgian pine cabinet provides handy storage, while a pine sofa table was made from vintage reclaimed wood. The room's vertical siding, added in the 1940s, was kept intact to emphasize the cottage look.

Built in 1910, the cottage had good bones with original six-over-six windows, square-mullioned doors, and the original heart-pine floors.

So it's not much of a surprise that when they were looking for a house they settled on a simple but charming bungalow in Birmingham's historic Homewood District. Built in 1910, the cottage had good bones with original six-over-six windows, square-mullioned doors, and the original heart-pine floors (hidden underneath new oak flooring).

Sited on a large, three-quarter-acre lot with a picturesque arbor in front, the cottage had room for Roy to indulge his passion for gardening. But since it was not spacious enough for their growing family of four children (all under the age of eleven), Roy and Becky devised a sympathetic addition for the cottage, adding three bedrooms and a bath. Every detail was so carefully thought out so that it's hard to tell the addition was recently built. Antique wooden shutters were used on the exterior to blend the new windows with the old, and the home's stone chimney was restored using a period photograph and cast reproduction stones that matched the originals exactly. The

Wrought-iron railing from Yorkshire, England, makes a perfect fireplace grille, its chipped, painted surface carefully left untouched to add to its vintage charm.

Right: The English Arts and Crafts oak mantel was added to replace the original, which had been removed. A Victorian Gothic door frame from an English church was mounted over the mantel, and small nineteenth-century clay pots were hung inside the frame. Some of Roy's favorite salvage finds displayed on the mantel include the weathered zinc roof finial and wooden dough bowls from England. Vintage green earthenware jugs and French wine bottles in their original baskets add a note of country French charm.

home's mantel had been removed, so Roy and Becky found an English oak substitute of the same period, keeping the charming, vertical board siding intact in the parlor. The siding, which had been added in the 1940s, was a wrinkle of the house, Roy points out, that they wanted to preserve.

Of course, favorite salvage pieces from the store soon made their way into the home. A fireplace grille fashioned from 1890s wrought-iron railing found in Yorkshire, England, guards the fireplace, while furniture in the parlor includes a pine table made from reclaimed wood from England. An arched Gothic door frame from an English Victorian church was elevated to a new status as an over-the-mantel

Old wooden balustrades from a demolished Southern plantation are given new life as candleholders on top of the built-in bookcase. The marble statue was found in England.

decoration and filled with Victorian terra-cotta pots. And a crusty zinc roof finial and wooden dough bowls were placed on the mantel below.

Furniture in the room was chosen to be practical and whimsical: Roy's grandfather's valise with stickers from his around-the-world travels now doubles as a side table, while a table lamp was fashioned from a wrought-iron finial, secured with a marble base. Balustrades from an early Southern plantation house were recycled as candlesticks and placed on top of a built-in bookcase.

In the dining room, the table was made from reclaimed flooring, one of Roy's shop's specialties, and decorated with more shop treasures, including a Victorian cast-iron chimney pot. A mixture of oak side chairs, durable enough for the children to use, were found at small English country antiques fairs and placed around the table. A 1940s American brass chandelier was found

A photograph of Roy's grandfather, a pilot in the 1920s, along with his binoculars, rests on a table lit by a lamp fashioned from salvaged wrought-iron railing found in Yorkshire, England.

in Birmingham, and an American pie safe was made into a bar. A concrete statue from the 1930s was placed in the corner of the dining room as a playful, decorative accent.

Roy and Becky made sure that even the children's rooms had an architectural artifact or two so they could learn to appreciate them while growing up. The baby's room has two stained-glass windows mounted on the wall, one of the first presents Becky gave Roy while they were still in college, while their son's room sports a colorful collection of old flags from countries around the world, along with a 1962 Austin Healy grille on the wall.

Roy has not only turned his passion for architectural salvage from a garage hobby into a successful, full-time career but also brought back to life a simple Southern cottage as well, using whimsical architectural pieces. Roy is just doing his part, he explains, in saving the best of the past for the future.

The dining room is centered on a large pine table made from reclaimed flooring, and lit overhead by a 1940s brass chandelier. More salvage on the table includes an unusual cast-iron chimney pot with its original verdigris surface. An assortment of sturdy side chairs found at English country sales was chosen for their practicality for the children. A pie safe in the corner has new life as a bar, and a whimsical concrete garden statue from the 1930s rests in the corner.

120

Roy and Becky's youngest child has been exposed to the beauty of salvage from a tender age, her room being decorated with a pair of Victorian stained-glass windows that Becky gave Roy while they were dating in college.

East Hampton Modern

Architect Michael Haverland and his partner, attorney and novelist Philip Galanes, had rented weekend homes in East Hampton for five years. They grew to love the picturesque Long Island coastline and the charming village of vernacular shingled homes. When they decided to build a weekend retreat of their own, a quiet getaway from their duplex in congested New York City, they found a secluded 1.1-acre lot on the edge of a forest preserve off the main village lanes.

Initially they envisioned a California Modern house, attracted by the openness of design. But then a trip to Paris and a visit to the Maison de Verre changed their minds. Built between 1927 and 1932 by Pierre Chareau, the "House of Glass" is an icon of Modern design constructed of glass, glass block and steel. Industrial elements, bare steel beams, rubberized floor tiles and industrial lighting are juxtaposed with more traditional home

Initially they envisioned a California Modern house, attracted by the openness of design. But a trip to Paris and a visit to the Maison de Verre changed their minds.

Opposite: A corner of the living room has an angular steel fireplace inspired by a Jean Prouve design. A pair of Florence Knoll armchairs, c. 1950, was covered in a period toile cotton print. A Little Tulip chair by Pierre Paulin still has its original knobby woven wool fabric. An Indian parchment lamp rests on the floor. The area rug, c. 1900, was found in Morocco. Notice the variation of color in the stuccoed walls that helps lend warmth and age to the room.

design for an honesty of construction and transparency of form. Inspired, the partners returned to New York and produced their own version of this famous modern home, theirs a glass box of exposed industrial steel beams and 12½-foot walls of glass (made of more practical insulated glass rather than the Maison de Verre's glass blocks).

Labor was divided: Michael devised the architectural plans and Philip designed the interiors. Rooms were kept open and the home's layout pulled apart; a patio, guest room and garage were distributed around the site with walls that extend from the inside out, making a series of outdoor rooms that are also screened from the sight of neighbors. Generous roof overhangs keep the interiors cool, and cross ventilation captures the breezes, making the house comfortable year-round. A rippling blue lap pool extending across the front patio makes the house appear to float on its site.

To soften the industrial starkness and add interest and detail, architectural

salvage was used throughout the home. A French country sink in the kitchen, windows cast from old factory window profiles, and vintage lighting—such as a pair of antique brass commercial chandeliers and a prismed globe from Paris—were found on foraging expeditions across the country. Warm palettes were chosen to add character to the home, the color of the woodwork throughout the house, for example, being taken from the golden oak finish on a pair of hundred-year-old pocket doors used for the library. Incorporating salvaged architecture with its charming variations and inconsistencies gave the house a warmth and forgiveness, Michael explains, that cannot be duplicated by new construction—

Inspired by the famous Maison de Verre ("House of Glass") built between 1927 and 1932 in Paris, the house was designed as a large glass box. Soaring 12½-foot-tall glass walls are framed with mullioned steel windows and doors, and the overall effect is one of an interior that blends seamlessly into the exterior of surrounding woodlands. Furniture is a mix of Modern movement designs, including a pair of Marco Zanuso armchairs upholstered in turquoise on the right, a Dunbar brown velour sofa, c. 1950, and a pair of Eames prototype leather side chairs. An Arredoluce Italian lamp from the 1940s provides lighting over the sofa. The chenille curtains and undercurtains of a sunblock fabric can be pulled across the glass walls for warmth in the evenings.

More salvage was used in the light and airy kitchen, including antique marble for the center island, c. 1900 milk glass lights, and a 1930s French country sink. Circa 1950s rosewood Eames chairs sit around a breakfast table fashioned from an Eames table base updated with a new travertine top. An Edward Fields area rug from the 1960s warms the tile floor. The contemporary cabinets are enlivened with decoupaged botanical prints.

although their most recent addition, a six-month-old miniature apricot poodle named Cichio, is doing his best to add his own layer of patina.

Entering the home you know it is going to be innovative: the front door, with an oversized Victorian brass door-knob in the center, turns on an asymmetrical, off-center pivot hinge. A short entry corridor opens directly into the central space of the home, essentially a giant glass rectangle. The glass walls, soaring to 12½ feet, are articulated with mullioned steel windows and doors opening to the outside. Minimal divisions between the rooms make the home feel spacious and grand. For instance, a freestanding screen covered in a William Morris wallpaper is the only element dividing the dining room from the kitchen and den. The high ceilings are punctuated with dropped chandeliers, such as an American commercial brass chandelier from the 1940s hung in the living room, and circa 1900 milk glass shades hung over the kitchen sink.

A pair of c. 1900 oak pocket doors was used to give the library character and age. A Jacques Adnet c. 1940 leather library desk and a Jean Prouvé Standard chair rest in front of built-in bookcases. This is where Philip edited his recently published novel, Father's Day.

127

The floors are covered with cool, chalk-colored
Turkish travertine floor tiles . . .

The floors are covered with cool, chalk-colored Turkish travertine floor tiles and accented with period rugs the partners collected on their travels. The windows are hung with tall, harvest-gold chenille curtains with separate liners of sun-block fabric to keep the rooms temperate throughout the year. Walls were stuccoed with a warm brown local sand that was mixed with gray concrete, exposing the aggregate colors to suggest age. Michael was pleased, he admits, when some of the stucco began showing stress cracks, giving the walls instant age and patina.

Furniture is a mix of Modern finds blended with old favorites. In the living room, a pair of Marco Zanuso 1950s armchairs found in Rome was updated with a period-appropriate turquoise textured wool. Philip, who has an interest in Modern-movement design, added a Little Tulip chair by Pierre Paulin, a Dunbar brown velour sofa circa 1950, and Eames prototype leather side chairs as well. He also found a Saarinen Womb chair and a Jean Prouve desk and chair for his study.

A gilded Victorian mirror with old wavy and smoky glass, vintage brass cup holders, and c. 1920s porcelain wall sconces complement the c. 1930 French farm sink in the second bathroom.

Right: The walls of the master bathroom were covered with shop-painted, water-resistant panels of Masonite, which were joined with mahogany strips for a nautical look. A red-lacquered Fornasetti side table holds soap next to the Victorian claw-foot tub. A 1930s French farm-kitchen sink and 1920s wall sconces from a New York apartment building were also added.

128

The kitchen, open to the main area of the home, is defined by a freestanding island of salvaged white marble. Contemporary cabinets were dressed up with decoupaged botanical prints, simply color-copied from a nineteenth-century horticulture book.

Whenever possible, salvage was used. An old oak fireplace mantel was cut down and recycled for a modern, angular steel fireplace inspired by Jean Prouve. The heavy steel doors throughout the home were softened with nineteenth-century Victorian brass doorknobs and kick locks. Both baths were designed with vintage sinks, cup holders, soap dishes and other accessories, but as much as the partners wanted to use vintage brass plumbing fixtures, practicality forced them to compromise.

Circa 1930 Anglepoise English wall sconces in shiny industrial chrome are now at home in the master bedroom, and one of the partners' favorite finds—the late Mary Kay's personal Pepto Bismol–pink lounge chair—was placed in the corner of the room. In fact, pink is used throughout the bedroom to help soften the space, including a baby pink 1940s chenille bedspread as well as linens and accessories. A pair of night tables was found at a local flea market and relacquered in a rosy red for an updated look, while a 1940s polychrome French sewing box was placed in front of the window as a colorful accent.

Salvage was used in the hall, as well. A pair of brass trivets circa 1960 found at an antiques mall in Palm Springs was refashioned into shades for wall sconces whose interplay of shadow and light on the walls provides an arresting accent.

Striking, innovative, and unexpected in the middle of a wooded glen, this extraordinary home is more than a homage to an icon of Modern design. It is a warm and personal environment, softened by the color and character of unique architectural salvage and shaped by the owners' exceptional vision and sense of design.

Vintage 1960s trivets found in a Palm Springs antiques mall were recycled into wall sconce shades. Their play of light and shadow create a striking accent in the hallway.

Right: The late Mary Kay's Pepto Bismol–pink lounge chair rests in a place of honor in the bedroom, which is decorated in rosy shades of pink and red, including a 1940s baby pink chenille bedspread. The Anglepoise chrome wall sconces are a classic industrial English design, c. 1930. Walls extending from the house into the yard define a private garden area.

Chelsea Conversion

Doron Sabag didn't start out designing homes. A banker, he was just looking for a comfortable apartment when he purchased the two neighboring fifth-floor walk-up apartments of an 1876 building in New York's Chelsea neighborhood. But by the time he had finished remodeling, Doron had had such an enjoyable experience that he decided to leave banking and begin his own real estate development firm, Sound Beach Partners (www.soundbeachpartners.com).

The Chelsea brownstone, once a gracious single-family residence, had been converted into co-op apartments and any original details had long ago been stripped away. Originally the maids' quarters, the two fifth-floor apartments had never been elaborate. So after purchasing both units, Doron decided to add a second story on top of them, opening the rooms up to light and views of the neighborhood. As the building is landmark-protected, this

After purchasing both units, Doron decided to add a second story on top of them, opening the rooms up to light and views of the neighborhood.

Opposite: An assortment of salvaged cabinets was used to make a unique and charming kitchen.

A Victorian walnut breakfront was converted into cabinets, accented with a nineteenth-century oil-lamp wall sconce.

Right: The Sub-Zero refrigerator is cleverly concealed behind old painted tin ceiling panels. The brass door pull is also vintage.

Opposite: The Art Deco pine-and-wrought-iron doors, imported from a Netherlands mansion, set the kitchen apart from the entry hall.

took over six months of public hearings, every detail requiring approval; the exterior color of the addition, for example, had to be painted a light gray to reflect the hazy skies above.

But once planning permission was granted, Doron began extensive remodeling. Rooms were taken down to the studs, wiring and plumbing were updated, and the ventilation was re-routed from the dropped ceilings, which were opened back up to their original twelve-foot heights. Doron wanted to create a unique space, one with a bit of grandeur, so designed a sweeping staircase leading upstairs to the new second story. Architectural salvage became an important element of the redesign, adding rich details and interest to the once-ordinary rooms. Doron found a set of massive pine-and-wrought-iron doors, originally from a mansion in the Netherlands, at an architectural salvage store and installed these as the entranceway to the kitchen. Details are what make the difference, and before new door casings were installed they were carefully distressed with screws and chains to make sure they matched the distressed vintage woodwork of the kitchen doors. A nineteenth-century walnut breakfront found at auction was used for the kitchen cabinets, while a pine cashier's table was cut down to house the kitchen sink. Lower cabinets were added and painted a soft gray with mustard yellow trim for a country French accent. And while Doron's updated appliances included a Sub-Zero refrigerator, he cleverly camouflaged it by covering the front with old painted tin ceiling panels and adding a period door pull. A glass-and-wrought-iron Moroccan light fixture found at the flea market added an exotic touch.

A marble mantel for the living room was found in twenty-two separate pieces and, like a giant jigsaw puzzle, was put back together and installed as the focal point of the living room. Once the dropped ceilings were removed, the living room windows were found to be disproportionately small; since Doron could not

Sadie, the owner's miniature collie, rests on the bed of the master bedroom. The soapstone mantel was salvaged from a dumpster. The room is painted in tones of green and gold to harmonize with the mantel.

Right: The living room is centered on a salvaged mantel. Note the shutters placed at the tops of the windows to give the illusion of taller openings. The French Empire table and chairs were found at auction.

alter their outline due to the exterior's landmark restrictions, he created wooden shutters with a faux panel on top to give the illusion of taller windows. An 1890s French gilded mirror was added over the mantel for an elegant touch.

More salvage was used throughout the apartment. Doron discovered a pair of immense, ten-foot-tall walnut doors while rollerblading one afternoon and ended up incorporating them as the master bedroom's closet doors. A vintage green soapstone mantel was found in a dumpster from the demolition of a brownstone in Harlem and installed in the bedroom, and a 1920s wire-mesh-and-abalone-shell shade was added for the overhead light fixture. The timeworn patina of the closet doors and variegated tones of the mantel glow in the mellow light of the room, which is painted a combination of soft sage green on the ceiling and warm, golden maize on the walls.

The 1,000-square-foot second-story addition fills the apartment with sunlight

that streams down from a handmade copper skylight above the stairs. The upstairs, a comfortable TV room and den, is surrounded on both sides by wide terraces built with old wooden porch columns found in Washington, D.C. Doron can indulge his love of gardening here and has filled both terraces with containers of brightly colored annuals, perennials, and shrubs.

Architectural artifacts have become an important part of Doron's life. His Chelsea conversion was so successful that he has now launched a second career designing and building homes with architectural salvage, creating unique and classic residences.

Wisteria winds over the trellis on the south terrace; the nineteenth-century wooden columns were found in Washington D.C. The owner's dog enjoys the fresh air.

Left: A pair of Victorian doors from a San Francisco mansion made perfect closet doors in the bedroom. The comfortable reading chair was found at auction.

Collector's Passion

Dr. Robert Lerch is blessed with a keen intellect, an inquisitive mind and a good eye—qualities that have served him well in his profession as a surgeon. And these same attributes have helped him fill his New York townhome with an extraordinary collection of architectural oddities and treasures, from cast-iron columns and ornate stained-glass windows and lamps to machines and manufactured objects that most people would pass over. Not many, for example, would give a second thought to cast-bronze bridge lamps from the 1930s, nineteenth-century figural pool table pockets or an old pharmacy jar for selling baby nipples. But Bob's visual acumen and sense of style have allowed him to discover the beauty and magic in other people's castaways, successfully gathering these very diverse objects together in an interesting and bemusing one-of-a-kind collection.

Bob has always had a passion for collecting. As a young boy, he filled his

Not many, for example, would give a second thought to cast-bronze bridge lamps from the 1930s, nineteenth-century figural pool table pockets or an old pharmacy jar for selling baby nipples.

Opposite: Filled with collections of architectural and advertising treasure, the upstairs living room is supported by salvaged nineteenth-century cast-iron columns. Circa 1930 bronze bridge lights form a division down the center of the room. The glazed terra-cotta fireplace came from a 1920s bank and was found buried in a backyard, and a c. 1910 shooting-gallery clown rests on the mantel top. Part of an extensive Bakelite jewelry collection is framed on the walls.

room with stamp collections, coins and rocks. By medical school he had begun to discover architectural antiques and started accumulating anything that caught his eye: rare mercury mosaic stained-glass windows, fancy Victorian fretwork and architectural columns, glazed terra-cotta panels from a bank. While he had no spot for them at the time, he knew that someday he would find a home to display them properly. So, by the time he purchased a five-story brownstone on New York's Upper East Side, he had an enviable architectural inventory from which to choose. The 1885 building was structurally sound but had been stripped clean of

A Victorian aquarium is mischievously filled with windup toy snails, c. 1940. The aquarium table, c. 1900, even has an aquatic theme with bronze seahorse supports; the frog lamp is Austrian, c. 1890.

A pair of oversized 1950s store-display glasses rests on top of a French steel paint-sample cabinet, c. 1930, in the upstairs living room. "The Old Mill" is a 1920s coin-operated vending machine, while a French vending machine, c. 1940, sits on the floor underneath.

Below: A 1920s cast-aluminum floor-model bank-deposit machine in the form of a bank building rests next to the fireplace.

original architectural elements—exactly what Bob wanted: a clean palette, that is, on which to display his treasures.

The building had been divided into apartments and an interior staircase was added in the back. For the first eleven months after they moved in, Bob, his wife and their daughter lived in one room and shared a bathroom with a construction crew while the entire house was renovated. The back staircase was removed, apartment walls were torn down, and modern baths and services were installed. As the building was returned to a single-family home, Bob stipulated that no new architectural details be added, no cove molding, columns or fancy lighting—he had his own supply.

Much as with a giant jigsaw puzzle, Bob found spots for everything. Since there were multiple collections to accommodate, cabinets and large shadow boxes were built to display like pieces together; the grouping of similar objects being a key principle in Bob's interior design.

Thus, one guest bath has glass shelves and cabinets built across two walls to display a colorful collection of German, Schaffer and Vater bisque figurine bottles from the early 1900s, while in the upstairs parlor large shadow boxes were constructed to hold part of Bob's massive Bakelite collection—thousands of pieces ranging from bracelets and buttons to napkin-ring holders.

A keen eye for unorthodox uses of objects is another of Bob's secrets for success. Ornate brass pool table pockets were recycled as candleholders, arranged up the lower wall of the staircase. Bob admits he has a weakness for brightly colored Bakelite radios from the second quarter of the twentieth century, and he grouped his collection of more than a hundred examples in every style and shape imaginable in simple, floor-to-ceiling, open shelving in the master bedroom; displayed together, the radios generate a power and presence that individually would be lost.

The dining room is paneled in American Aesthetic movement dressing-room screens recycled into wall panels and surrounded by walnut Aesthetic movement chairs. A Tiffany octopus lamp hangs over the dining table, which is custom made with cast-iron pool table legs of elephant heads and trunks. A c. 1930 coin-operated vending machine for dispensing fruitcake rests in the center of the table. An Austrian bronze-and-jeweled table lamp in the form of peacocks sits on a table in the corner.

Left: Aluminum bas-relief panels of Art and Music were hung above the bed in the master bedroom. A 1905 cast-iron Mickey Finn strength tester rests in the corner; next to it is a c. 1900 cast-iron jewelry store sign in the form of a woman. A pair of 1940s beauty parlor gas heaters in the form of large "Mermaid" and "Merman" seashells rests between a Black Forest trunk at the foot of the bed.

Cast-brass figural pool pockets have been given new life as candlelit sconces along the stairs. Never one to take himself too seriously, the owner adds a wry note of humor with the early-twentieth-century leather and nickel-bronze prosthetic arms holding a pool ball.

Left: The opposite side of the master bedroom is centered on a fireplace made around a set of copper-plated iron elevator panels and beveled mirrors. The Austrian chandelier supports a bronze alligator with jewels inset in its back. Clown target figures rest on the mantel. A collection of Bakelite radios is displayed on simple open shelves across the back of the room.

A guest bath is fitted with an Arts and Crafts mirror, c. 1900, and a figural downspout from Antwerp. The chrome dolphin on the floor is from a 1930s amusement park, while the frosted lamps on the windowsill are novelty circus lights. Several Schaffer and Vater figural bottles rest on the shelf above the sink, and many more are displayed in glass cabinets on the opposite wall.

cast-iron strength tester rests in the corner. A pair of jewel-faceted, cast-iron gas heaters in the shape of large "Mermaid" and "Merman" seashells, taken from a 1940s beauty parlor, sit in front of the bed and have now been converted into night-lights.

Buy what amuses you, Bob advises, and trust your natural eye and instincts. Architectural salvage has a hidden charisma all its own that when properly appreciated becomes as beautiful as a fine painting or work of art.

A nineteenth-century figural cast-iron sink with winged griffins rests on the opposite side of the master bath.

Top left: An early-twentieth-century pharmacy jar for selling bottle nipples rests on the bathroom windowsill and is filled with 1920s toy tin mice. The motto on the jar reads, "No other nipple gives equal satisfaction."

Above: A sunken tub in the master bathroom is accented with a striking 1940s wrought-iron panel of a silhouetted speakeasy dancer. Early-twentieth-century cast-iron facial molds for growing pumpkins rest around the rim of the tub.

Left: The mantel shelf is decorated with a seahorse bronze frieze from a Victorian aquarium, a French bronze praying mantis lamp with a chunk jewel shade that once belonged to Barbra Streisand, and an Austrian bronze-and-glass frog jar, c. 1900.

150

The living room is furnished
with a variety of unusual
architectural treasures,
including a salvaged marble
mantel and a large Tiffany
turtleback globe overhead.
The 1888 painting by
Vellamy above the mantel is
titled The Flood *and depicts
the end of the world.*

Architectural Salvage Companies—by Name

A & O Architectural Salvage
Doors, stained glass and windows, lighting, mantels, terra cotta, more
2045 Broadway, Kansas City, MO 64108
Telephone: 816-283-3740
Fax: 816-421-6799
Web site: www.aoarchitecturalsalvage.com

A & R Salvage
Home and commercial salvaged and recycled building materials. Plumbing fixtures, woodwork, vintage architectural salvage items, doors, windows, hardware, light fixtures, wrought iron
2820 Vinton Street, Omaha, NE 68105
Telephone: 402-346-4470
Web site: www.arsalvage.com
E-mail: sales@arsalvage.com

Aardvark Antiques
Interior and exterior architecturals, fine furniture, antique stained glass, lighting, antique rugs, garden accents, iron gates and fencing
4616 Mundy Mill Road, Oakwood, GA 30566
Telephone: 770-534-6611
1740 Cleveland Hwy., Gainesville, GA 30501
Telephone: 770-531-1665
Web site: www.aardvark-antiques.com
E-mail: charles@aardvark-antiques.com

Ace Demolitions Center
Reclaimed timber of all sizes, cast iron fire inserts, wood and marble fire surrounds, paneling, chimney pots, column radiators, roll-top baths; flag stones, pavers, cobbles, roof tiles, antique bricks
Michelle Randle, Barrack Road, West Parley, Wimbourne, Dorset, BH22 8UB.
Telephone: +44 (0) 1202-579222
Website: www.acedemo.co.uk

Adkins Architectural Antiques
Antiques, repairs, restorations, custom work; sales and rentals
Doors, mantles, hardware, lighting, stained glass, architectural artifacts, plumbing and bath, weather vanes, garden decor, fountains, odds & ends
3515 Fannin Street, Houston, TX 77004
Telephone: 713-522-6547; 800-522-6547
Web site: www.adkinsantiques.com
E-mail: adkins@adkinsantiques.com

Admac Salvage
Doors, windows, leaded and stained glass, mantels, porch parts, lighting, period hardware and plumbing fixtures, claw-foot tubs, slate, marble, brick
111 Saranac Street, Littleton, NH 03561
Telephone: 603-444-1200
Fax: 603-444-1211
Web site: www.admacsalvage.com
E-mail: admac@ncia.net

Advanced Refinishing
Bathtubs: buy, sell, restore
Specializing in claw-foot and pedestal tubs, reproduction plumbing fixtures, everything for antique bathrooms Restore all types of bathtubs
Rochelle, IL 61068
Telephone: 877-562-8468
Web site: www.advancedrefinishing.com
E-mail: sales@advancedrefinishing.com

Affordable Antique Bath & More
Antiques, reproductions; plumbing fixtures, claw-foot tubs, pedestal sinks, faucets, pull-chain toilets, shower rods, other
3888 De Sabla Road, Cameron Park, CA 95682
Telephone: 888-303-2284, 530-677-9121
Fax: 530-677-1413
Web site: www.bathandmore.com
E-mail: sales@bathandmore.com

Aged Woods / Yesteryear Floorworks Co.
Antique and recycled wood: tongue-&-groove plank flooring, wide board, random width, timber framing, paneling, moldings, stair parts
2331 East Market Street, Suite 6, York, PA 17402
Telephone: 717-840-0330; 800-233-9307
Fax: 717-840-1468
Web site: www.agedwoods.com
E-mail: info@agedwoods.com

Airport Lumber Company
Architectural salvage, functional to decorative items
6222 W. Plank Road, Suite 1, Peoria, IL 61604-7213
Telephone: 309-697-1106

Al Bar-Wilmette Platers
Restoration/Repair/Refinishing of antique hardware and metal fixtures - all metals; match any finish; refurbish locks, large selection of salvage door hardware and light fixtures
127 Green Bay Road, Wilmette, IL 60091
Telephone: 866-823-8404
Fax: 847-251-0281
Web site: www.albarwilmetteplaters.com
E-mail: info@albarwilmette.com

Albany Woodworks
Custom fabricator of architectural millwork, plank flooring, custom doors, plantation shutters, exposed beams, stair parts; woods include antique heart pine, virgin tidewater cypress, NuHeart pine, and American hardwoods
P.O. Box 729, Albany, LA 70711
Telephone: 800-551-1282; 225-567-1155
Fax: 225-567-5150
Web site: www.albanywoodworks.com
E-mail: woods@i-55.com

All Around Demolition Co. Ltd.
Reclamation yard, also demolition contractor
4912 Still Creek Avenue, Burnaby, V5C 4E4, British Columbia
Telephone: 604-299-2967
Fax: 604-299-1383

All the Things You Love
Architectural antiques, garden items, interior decorating
527 Bouthillier Street, Galena, IL 61036
Telephone: 815-777-8400
Fax: 815-777-8484
E-mail: designs@galenalink.net

Allie's Enterprizes
Auctions
RR 5, Box 1500, Gardiner, ME 04345
Telephone: 207-582-4661
Web site: www.alliesenterprizes.com
E-mail: alliesenterpriz@aol.com

Allison's Architectural Antique Salvage
Doors, mirrors, chandeliers, wood flooring, antique furnishings, decorative items
5716 Georgia Ave, West Palm Beach, FL 33405
Telephone: 561-582-2224

Amazing Glaze Restorations
Refinishing tubs, sinks, tile, anything porcelain
252 Cornwall Ave., Grass Valley, CA 95945
Telephone: 530-272-9000
E-mail: brad@shinytub.com

American Antique and Specialty Woods
Antique/reclaimed/recycled: wide plank flooring, hand-hewn beams; superior antique wood products—custom furniture, cabinetry, moldings, millwork, architecturally paneled rooms, stairs, and more; wide range of North American species
51 Mt. Bethel Road, Warren, NJ 07059
Telephone: 908-822-0006
Fax: 908-822-7111
Web site: www.dr-woods.com
E-mail: americanwoods@yahoo.com

American Salvage, Inc.
Architectural salvage of historical buildings, offices and hotels; sales and rentals
7001 and 9200 NW 27th Avenue, Miami, FL 33147
Telephone: 305-691-7001
Fax: 305-691-0001
Web site: www.americansalvage.com

American Timbers, LLC
Lumber recyclers
P.O. Box 430, Canterbury, CT 06331
Telephone: 800-461-8660
Fax: 860-546-9334
Web site: www.americantimbers.com
E-mail: sales@americantimbers.com

Amighini Architectural Inc.
Imported architectural items from different parts of the world; wholesale also wooden doors, windows, cupolas, stained glass, iron pieces, antique tiles, balconies, marble and cast-iron fireplaces, bronze and crystal lighting, garden accents, tiles, panels & fence, more
246 Beacon Avenue, Jersey City, NJ 07306
Telephone: 201-222-6367
Fax: 201-222-6368
Web site: www.amighini.net
E-mail: info@amighini.net

Antiquarian Traders
Sales and rentals; eBay sales
Restored antiques, custom modifications: architecturals, bars, furniture, lighting, mantels, mirrors, pedestals, stained glass, statuary, fine art and accent pieces, more
9031 West Olympic Blvd., Beverly Hills, CA 90211
Telephone: 310-247-3900
Fax: 310-247-8864
Web site: www.antiquariantraders.com
E-mail: info@AntiquarianTraders.com

Antique Market
Stained glass, architectural iron, lighting, chimney pots, furniture, architectural items
4280 Main Street, Vancouver, BC, Canada, V5V 3P9
Telephone: 604-875-1434
Web site: www.antiquemarket.com
E-mail: info@antiquemarketvancouver.com

Antiques Forain
Doors, windows, plumbing fixtures, stonework, fountains, urns, statues, chalets, wrought iron
35, rue Central Albigny 74940 Annecy-le-vieux, Haute-Savoie, France
Telephone: +33 (0) 4.50.23.68.13
Website: www.antiques-forain.com
e-mail: contact@antiques.forain.com

Appalachian Woods Antique Flooring
Specializing in antique wood flooring and lumber. Wide plank flooring, antique wood—oak, chestnut, heart pine, other woods; lumber, flooring, custom sawing, furniture, log cabins,
1240 Cold Springs Road, Stuarts Draft, VA 24477
Telephone: 540-337-1801; 800-333-7610
Fax: 540-337-1030
Web site: www.appalachianwoods.com
E-mail: AW@AppalachianWoods.com

Architectural Accents
Antiques and reproductions; doors, mantels, lighting, columns, hardware, bath, ironwork, tile, garden, glass
2711 Piedmont Road NE, Atlanta GA
Telephone: 404-266-8700
Fax: 404-266-0074

Architectural Salvage Companies—by Name (continued)

Web site: www.architecturalaccents.com
E-mail: info@architecturalaccents.com

Architectural Antique Warehouse
Doors, hardware, stained & beveled glass, mantels, lighting, bath fixtures, gates, fencing, posts, pillars, garden ornaments
17985 Highway 27, Fairhope, AL 36532
Telephone: 251-928-2880
Web site: www.Architectural-Antiques.com

Architectural Antiques (CO)
(also FL and MN)
Architectural antiques: ecclesiastical items, claw-foot tubs, hardware, lighting, other
2669 Larimer Street, Denver, CO 80205
Telephone: 303-297-9722
Fax: 303-297-9290
Web site: www.archantiques.com
E-mail: info@ArchAntiques.com

Architectural Antiques (MN)
Doors, windows, mantles, cabinetry, original hardware, vintage lighting, ecclesiastical artifacts
1330 Quincy Street NE, Minneapolis, MN 55413
Telephone: 612-332-8344
Fax: 612-332-8967
Web site: www.archantiques.com
E-mail: info@ArchAntiques.com

Architectural Antiques Exchange
Antique and reproduction mantels and doors, bars, furniture, stained glass, paneled rooms, lighting, ironwork, mirrors, paneling, artifacts
715 N. 2nd Street, Philadelphia, PA 19123
Telephone: 215-922-3669
Fax: 215-922-3680
Web site: www.architecturalantiques.com
E-mail: aaexchange@aol.com

Architectural Antiquities
Doors, windows, stained glass, fireplace items, lighting, Victorian plumbing fixtures, hardware
Harborside, ME 04642
Telephone: 207-326-4938
Web site: www.archantiquities.com
E-mail: sales@archantiquities.com

Architectural Artifacts (CO)
Doors, mantels, lighting fixtures, tin ceilings, restored claw-foot tubs & pedestal sinks, hardware
2207 Larimer Street, Denver, CO 80205
Telephone: 303-292-6012
Telephone (salvage yard): 303-296-0925
Fax: 303-403-0886
Web site: www.architectural-artifacts.com

Architectural Artifacts (OH)
(Architectural Artifacts & Antiques)
Lighting, fountains, statuary, ornamental trees, antiques, ironwork, fireplace elements
20 South Ontario Street, Toledo, OH 43602

Telephone: 419-243-6916
Fax: 419-243-0094

Architectural Artifacts, Inc. (IL)
No reproductions
Stained glass, doors, fireplace mantels, period lighting, tiles, garden furnishings, cast & wrought iron, carved stone, furniture, religious artifacts
4325 Ravenswood, Chicago, IL 60613
Telephone: 773-348-0622
Web site: www.architecturalartifacts.com

Architectural Clearinghouse
Used building materials
5920 103 Street NE, Edmonton, AB T6H 2H6
Telephone: 780-436-1222
Fax: 780-436-9345

Architectural Elements
Doors, windows, fireplace mantles, light fixtures, wrought iron, much more. Local and regional sources
2202 E. Admiral Boulevard, Tulsa, OK 74110
Telephone: 877-506-7950, 918-382-7950
Web site: www.arc-elements.com
E-mail: arc-elements@juno.com

Architectural Exchange
Doors, windows, stained glass, architecturals, custom flooring
1300 McCallie Avenue, Chattanooga, TN 37404
Telephone: 423-697-1243
Web site:
www.mywebpages.comcast.net/tnhotairpilot/archex/index.html

Architectural Heritage
Doors, mantels, lighting, garden, statuary, decorative items
2807 Second Avenue South, Birmingham, AL 35233
Telephone: 205-322-3538
Fax: 205-323-0084
Web site: www.architecturalheritage.com
E-mail: Laura@architecturalheritage.com

Architectural Salvage (CA)
Stained-glass doors and windows, furniture, lighting, vintage household goods
1971 India St., San Diego, CA 92101
Telephone: 619-696-1313
Fax: 619-696-7759

Architectural Salvage (LA)
Antique doors, mantles, windows, columns, corbels, brackets, flooring, light fixtures, stained glass, decorative elements, and cypress and iron furniture
410 Covington Street, Madisonville, LA 70420
Telephone: 985-845-8455
Fax: 985-845-8455
Web site: www.architectural-salvage.net

E-mail: justmejunkin@yahoo.com

Architectural Salvage by Ri-Jo
Doors, mantels, columns, posts, lighting, plumbing fixtures
2309 Highway 71 South, Mena, AR 71953
Telephone: 479-394-2438
E-mail: salvage@arkansas.net

Architectural Salvage, Inc.
Doors, windows, mantels, stair parts, flooring, lighting, bath fixtures, floor registers, iron work, complete doorways, molding and extensive hardware
3 Mill Street, Exter, NH 03833
Telephone: 603-773-5635
Fax: 603-773-5635
Web site: www.oldhousesalvage.com

Architectural Salvage, W.D. Inc.
Doors, reproduction mahogany entryways, leaded glass, mantels, light fixtures, plumbing fixtures, hardware, ironwork, chimney tops, stonework, yard and garden items, custom fabrication from antique iron pieces
614 - 618 E. Broadway, Louisville, KY 40201
Telephone: 502-589-0670
Fax: 502-589-4024
Web site: www.architecturalsalvage.com
E-mail: info@architecturalsalvage.com

Architectural Salvage Warehouse (VT)
Mantels, doors, windows, hardware, plumbing, lighting, columns, posts, corbels, miscellaneous; we also buy salvage rights to older businesses
53 Main Street, Burlington, VT 05401
Telephone: 802-658-5011
Web site: www.architecturalsalvagevt.com
E-mail: jon@greatsalvage.com

Architectural Timber & Millwork
Restorations, antique materials and supplies, timber structural systems, houses and barns
49 Mount Warner Road, P.O. Box 719, Hadley, MA 01035
Telephone: 413-586-3045, 800-430-5473
Fax: 413 586-3046
Web site: www.atimber.com
E-mail: info@atimber.com

Architecture & Materiaux Authentiques
Doors, mantels, flooring, tiles, plumbing fixtures, wrought iron, carved stone
212, rue du Flocon - 59200 Tourcoing
Telephone: +33 (0) 3.20.68.01.01
Website: www.materiauxauthentiques.com
e-mail: pomaster@materiauxauthentiques.com

Architiques
Architectural salvage, antiques, home accents
35 Otsego Street, Oneonta, NY 13820
Telephone: 607-432-9890

Fax: 607-432-4119
Web site: www.architiques.net
E-mail: elm@stny.rr.com

Armadillo-South Architectural Salvage, Inc.
Doors and entryways, millwork, windows, mantles, fencing, lumber, bath tubs, bricks, marble, fencing and gates, cypress beams, roof tiles, antique slate, more
4801 Washington Avenue, New Orleans, LA 70125
Telephone: 504-486-1150
Fax: 504-324-6890
Web site: www.armadillo-south.com
E-mail: sales@armadillo-south.com

Artefacts
Architectural antiques: Doors, panels, windows, lighting, hinges, interior and exterior architectural details, decorative tiles, cast & wrought iron
17 King St., St. Jacobs, N0B 2N0, Ontario
Telephone: 519-664-3760
Fax: 519-664-1303

Auctionsales.ca
Auction catalogues of livestock through salvage and antiques
Saskatoon, Saskatchewan
Telephone: 306-373-2236
Fax: 306-373-4244
Web site: www.auctionsales.ca

Aurora Lampworks
Restoration, reproduction of historical and custom lighting fixtures
172 N. 11th Street, Brooklyn, NY 11211
Telephone: 718-384-6039
Fax: 718-384-6198
Web site: www.auroralampworks.com
E-mail: ask@auroralampworks.com

Aurora Mills Architectural
Doors, windows, woodwork, lighting, bath fixtures, hardware, ironwork, garden decor
14971 First Street, Aurora, OR 97002
Telephone: 503-678-6083
Web site: www.auroramills.com

Authentic Provence
Reproduction marble and limestone fountains, mantels, garden ornaments, architectural elements
522 Clematis Street, West Palm Beach, FL 33401
Telephone: 561-805-9995; Fax: 561-805-5730
Web site: www.authenticprovence.com
E-mail: info@authenticprovence.com

Ball and Ball
Antique hardware reproductions: door, window, shutter & furniture hardware, fireplace tools; wrought iron/steel, bronze, brass, copper, cast iron; custom reproductions
463 W. Lincoln Highway, Exton, PA 19341
Telephone: 610-363-7330
Fax: 610-363-7639
Web site: www.ballandball-us.com
E-mail: bill@ballandball-us.com

Balleycanoe and Co.
Doors, windows, mantels, gingerbread, iron, stairway components, hardware, brackets, tin
150 Rockfield Road, Mallorytown, Ontario, Canada, K0E 1R0
Telephone: 613-659-3874
Web site: www.balleycanoe.com

Ballyalton House Architectural Antiques
Leaded and stained glass, doors and door furniture, door and window surrounds, beams, flooring, sandstone and granite steps, bricks, building stones, pavers, cobbles, tiles, kerbs, extensive garden elements
39 Ballyrainey Road, Newtownards, Co Down, BT23 5AD, Northern Ireland
Telephone: +44 (0) 2891-813235
Website: www.ballyalton.freeserve.co.uk
e-mail: andrew@ballyalton.freeserve.co.uk

The Barn People
Vintage barns dismantled and reassembled; consulting, restoration, preservation
2218 US Route 5, Windsor, VT 05089
Telephone: 802-674-5898
Fax: 802-674-6310
Web site: www.thebarnpeople.com

Bedford Salvage Company
Leaded and stained-glass windows, interior and exterior doors, mantels, corbels, lighting, urns, more
2 Depot Plaza, Bedford Hills, NY 10507
Telephone: 914-666-4595
Web site: www.bedfordsalvage.com
E-mail: info@bedfordsalvage.com

Belcour
European and American fireplace surrounds, mantels, antique lighting, columns, stone and marble garden items, architectural elements and unique objects
1740 South Broadway, Denver, CO 80210
Telephone: 303-765-5151
Fax: 303-765-5252
Web site: www.belcour.net
E-mail: info@belcour.net

Blackbrook Antiques Village
Comprehensive range of building materials, plus fully restored chimney pieces and fireside items, antique lighting, stained glass, doors, bathroom fittings, outdoor/garden elements, selected architectural antiques and decorative items
London Road, Weeford (nr Lichfield), Staffordshire, WS14 0PS
Telephone: +44 (0) 1543-481450
Fax: +44 (0) 1543-480275
Website: www.blackbrook.co.uk
e-mail: info@blackbrook.co.uk

Black Dog Salvage
Mantles, doors, stained glass, lighting, ceiling tin, vintage plumbing, claw-foot tubs, architectural elements, decorative iron, custom designs
902 13th Street SW, Roanoke, VA 24016
Telephone: 540-343-6200
Fax: 540-343-6295
Web site: www.blackdogsalvage.com
E-mail: info@blackdogsalvage.com
eBay store: http://stores.ebay.com/Black-Dog-Architectural-Salvage

Blue Moon Salvage
Doors, windows, stained glass, mantles, radiators, columns, cabinets, bathroom fixtures, hardware, tin ceilings, marble, wrought iron, furniture
15 Depot Street, Rumney, NH 03266
Telephone: 603-786-2222
Web site: www.bluemoondalvage.com
E-mail: info@bluemoonsalvage.com

The Brass Knob
Mantels, extensive lighting, stained glass, hardware, decorative items
2311 18th Street NW, Washington, DC 20009
Telephone: 202-332-3370
Fax: 202-332-5594
Web site: thebrassknob.com
E-mail: bk@thebrassknob.com

The Brass Knob's Back Doors Warehouse
Doors, bathtubs, sinks, radiators, iron fencing, larger decorative architectural elements
2329 Champlain Street NW, Washington, DC 20009
Telephone: 202-265-0587

Bygones Architectural Reclamation (Canterbury) Ltd.
Doors , windows, stained glass, comprehensive fireplace items, lighting, radiators and parts, church items, roof finials, street signs, railway sleepers, garden elements, much more; also repairs and restorations
Nackington Road, Canterbury, Kent, CT4 7BA
Telephone: +44 (0) 1227-767453
Website: www.bygones.net

Caravati's, Inc.
Doors, windows, shutters, stained glass, mantels, columns, stairway components, plumbing fixtures, flooring, lighting, beams, roofing slate, more
104 East 2nd St., Richmond, VA 23224
Telephone: 804-232-4175
Fax: 804 233 7109
Web site: www.recentruins.com

Carlisle Wide Plank Floors
Manufacturer of traditional wide-plank floors: wide board and random width; antique and new wood; old growth pines, old growth hardwoods
1676 Route 9, Stoddard, NH 03464
Telephone: 800-595-9663
Web site: www.wideplankflooring.com
E-mail: info@wideplankflooring.com

Carlson's Barnwood Co.
Barnwood, tin, salvaged materials, antiques, antique wood flooring
8066 N. 1200 Ave., Cambridge, IL 61238
Telephone: 309-522-5550
Fax: 309-522-5123
Web site: www.carlsonsbarnwood.com
E-mail: info@carlsonbarnwood.com

Carolina Architectural Salvage @ Cogan's Antiques
Antique stained glass windows, doors, lighting, posts and columns, sinks, tubs, hardware, mantels, fireplace accessories, ironwork, Victorian furniture, architectural items
110 South Palmer Street, Ridgeway, SC 29130
Telephone: 803-337-3939
Web site: www.CogansAntiques.com
E-mail: John@CogansAntiques.com

Chen Ragan, LLC
Architectural elements, bamboo, stone and pottery, garden items
2100 East Union Street, Seattle, WA 98122
Telephone: 206-325-2456
Fax: 206-325-7779
Web site: www.chenragan.com
E-mail: info@chenragan.com.com

The Chimney Pot Shoppe
New and antique chimney pots, crafted in USA and imported from England
1915 Bush Run Road, Avella, PA 15312
Telephone: 724-345-3601
Fax: 724-345-8243
Web site: www.chimneypot.net
E-mail: bentley@chimneypot.net

City Lights Antique Lighting
Antique American and European light fixtures—many types and styles
2226 Massachusetts Avenue, Cambridge, MA 02140
Telephone: 617-547-1490
Fax: 617-479-2-74
Web site: www.citylights.nu
E-mail: lights@citylights.nu

City Salvage—Architectural Salvage and Antiques
American only. Stained glass, lighting, mantles, millwork, plumbing fixtures, furniture, other architecturals
505 1st Ave NE., Minneapolis, MN 55413-2209
Telephone: 612-627-9107
Web site: www.citysalvage.com
E-mail: mail@citysalvage.com

Cityscape Properties
Architectural salvage: doors, mantels, brackets, porch parts, unusual items, custom fabrication
49 South 14th Street, Pittsburgh, PA
Telephone: 412-481-8960
Web site: www.nauticom.net/www/cityscpe/index.html
E-mail: cityscpe@nauticom.net

Cook County Demolition Sales
Demolition site: Cook County, IL
Telephone: 847-795-9139
Web site: www.demolitionsales.com

Cornerstone
Limestone, antique wood, antique terra cotta, architectural elements, garden
499 Van Brunt St., Warehouse #8A, Brooklyn, NY 11231
Telephone: 718-782-3056
Fax: 718-486-6621
Web site: www.cornerstonesalvage.com
E-mail: amanda@cornerstonesalvage.com

Cottage Castle Homes
Copper roofing, louvers, finials, cupolas, and chimney pots; slate roofing and flooring, stone columns and surrounds, antique wood beams and flooring, wood corbels and molding
137 E. Highway "CC", Nixa, MO 67514-9396
Telephone: 417-725-6500

Country Image Antiques
Antique and reclaimed materials
404b Ogilvie Street, Whitehorse, Y1A 2S4, Yukon
Telephone: 867-667-7791
E-mail: pmorgan@yknet.yk.ca

Crescent City Architecturals
Doors, floors, windows, shutters, woodwork, accessories, ironwork
3033 Tchoupitoulas Street, New Orleans, LA 70115
Telephone: 877-245-0500
Web site: www.architectural-salvage.com

Crown City Hardware
Antique and restoration hardware: glass knobs, bin pulls, hinges, hooks, window/cabinet/bath hardware; iron, brass, glass & crystal; original antique hardware
1047 North Allen Ave., Pasadena, CA 91104
Telephone: 626-794-0234

Architectural Salvage Companies (continued)

Fax: 626-794-2064
Web site: www.crowncityhardware.com
E-mail: questions@restoration.com

Cunningham Lumber
Antique reclaimed lumber, old and specialty
woods, architecturals, custom metalwork
P O Box 976, Hillsboro, TX 76645
Telephone: 254-582-3089; 800-317-3089
Fax: 254-582-3684
Web site: www.cunninghamlumber.com
E-mail: tckc45@hotmail.com

DEA Bathroom Machineries
Bathroom fixtures & accessories: antique &
reproduction claw-foot tubs, high-tank toilets,
pedestal sinks, original light fixtures, medicine
cabinets, mirrors & many one-of-a-kind items
495 Main Street, Murphys, CA 95247
Telephone: 209-728-2031
Fax: 209-728-2320
Web site: www.deabath.com

Decodame.Com
Art deco and art nouveau architectural artifacts
and antiques: doors, woodwork, mantels,
lighting, hardware, ironwork, statuary, garden
items
Online sales only
Mailing address: 853 Vanderbilt Beach Road,
PMB #8, Naples, FL 34108
Web site: www.decodame.com
E-mail: Info@decodame.com

DHS Designs
Period mantels, garden items, continental furni-
ture, decorative arts
8521 Friel Road, Queenstown, MD 21658
Telephone: 410-827-8167
Web site: www.dhsdesigns.com

Door Store
Architectural antiques and ironwork, custom
and vintage, ornamental ironwork, salvaged
doors, mantelpieces, antique and reproduction hardware, unusual artifacts
1260 Castlefield Avenue, Toronto, Ontario M6B
1G3
Telephone 416-863-1590
Fax: 416-863-5088

Doors of London
British architectural antiques and reproductions;
items shipped directly from the U.K. to buyer
10903 Terrace Drive, Forestville, CA 95436
Telephone: 707-849-8972
Web site: www.doorsoflondon.com
E-mail: sales@doorsoflondon.com

Duluth Timber Company
Reclaimed flooring, posts, beams, paneling, siding; heart pine, jarrah, white pine, eucalyptus,
redwood, cypress
P.O. Box 16717, Duluth, MN 55816

Telephone: 218-727-2145
Fax: 218-727-0393
Web site: www.duluthtimber.com
E-mail: liz@duluthtimber.com

Earthwise
Lighting, mantles, stained glass, doors, cabinets, tile, bathroom fixtures, radiators, windows, hardware, plumbing, pillars, flooring,
moldings, more
2462 First Avenue South, Seattle, WA 98134
Telephone: 206-624-4510
Web site: www.earthwise-salvage.com
E-mail: earthwise@qwest.net

Ed Donaldson Hardware Restoration
Old and vintage hardware, restored antique hard-
ware, new parts and pieces, Victorian locks
1488 North Road, Carlisle, PA 17013
Telephone: 717-249-3624
Fax: 717-249-5647
Web site: www.eddonaldson.com
E-mail: ed@eddonaldson.com

**Edinburgh Architectural Salvage Yard
(EASY)**
Doors, windows, etched & stained glass, shutters, lighting, fire surrounds, radiators, roll-
top cast iron baths, plumbing fixtures and
hardware, benches, lamp posts, balconies,
balustrades, decorative columns, carriage
gates, more
Edinburgh, Lothian
Telephone: +44 (0) 1315-547077
Website: www.easy-arch-salv.co.uk

English Antique Imports
Antique chimney pots, architectural items, garden
features and statuary, furniture, butler's sinks
North Carolina Highway 105, Banner Elk, NC
28604
P.O. Box 2302, Boone, NC 28607
Telephone: 828-963-4274, 888-768-8677
Web site: www.englishantiqueimports.com

Eron Johnson Antiques, Ltd.
Doors, fireplaces, capitals, fireplaces and
accessories, stained glass, windows, iron
doors/gates/arches/ transoms, other architec-
tural pieces
451 Broadway, Denver, CO 80203
Telephone: 303-777-8700
Fax: 303-777-8787
Web site: www.antiques-internet.com
E-mail: eron@eronjohnsonantiques.com

Eugenia's Antique Hardware
Door knockers, hinges, door plates, rosettes,
twist bells, furniture and bathroom hardware
5370 Peachtree Road, Chamblee, Georgia, 30341
Telephone: 800-337-1677; 770-458-5966
Fax: 770-458-5966
Web site: www.eugeniaantiquehardware.com
E-mail: eugeniashardware@mindspring.com

Exploits Salvage
Demolition salvage
68 Whitmire, Grand Falls, NF, A2B 1B8,
Newfoundland and Labrador
Telephone: 866-489-1170

FIFI's House Parts and Salvage
Windows, doors, cupboards and cabinets, light-
ing, Victorian wood work trim, slate roofing
North Belfast Avenue, Augusta, ME 04330
Telephone and fax: 207-623-0434
Web site: www.fifisalvage.com
E-mail: fifi@fifisalvage.com

Florida Victorian Architectural Antiques
Antique building materials: doors, windows,
wood flooring, mantels, hardware, ornamental
iron, lighting, bathroom fixtures, vintage gar-
den items, movie and TV props
112 W. Georgia Avenue, DeLand, FL 32720
Telephone: 386-734-9300
Fax: 386-734-1150
Web site: www.floridavictorian.com
E-mail: info@floridavictorian.com

Garden Park Antiques
Architectural & garden antiques: ironwork,
windows, doors, shutters, mantels, brackets,
pediments, miscellaneous
7121 Cockrill Bend Blvd., Nashville, TN 37209
Telephone: 615-350-6655
Fax: 615-350-6471
Web site: www.gardenpark.com
E-mail: info@gardenpark.com

Gavin Historical Brick
Antique brick, granite cobblestones, clinker
brick, brick pavers and flooring, limestone
2050 Glendale Road, Iowa City, IA 52245
Telephone: 319-354-5251
Web site: www.historicalbricks.com
E-mail: info@historicalbricks.com

Good Time Stove Co.
Authentic antique kitchen ranges and heating
stoves, fully restored and functional: enamel,
cast iron, wood, wood-gas combos, conver-
sions available
188A Cape Street, Goshen, MA 01032
Telephone: 413-268-3677
Web site: www.goodtimestove.com
E-mail: stoveprincess@goodtimestove.com

Great Gatsby's
Entryways, stained glass, mantels, gazebos,
garden elements, iron gates, more
5070 Peachtree Industrial Blvd., Atlanta, GA
303412
Telephone: 800-428-7297; 770-457-1903
Fax: 770-457-7250
Web site: www.greatgatsbys.com
E-mail: sales@greatgatsbys.com

Grindstone
Reclamation yard; associate "Happy Harry" store
140 Caledonia Road, Moncton, New Brunswick
Telephone: 506-855-7999
Fax: 506-364-1985

Happy Harry's Used Building Materials
Reclamation yard
46 Wright Avenue, Dartmouth, Nova Scotia B3B 1G6
Phone: 902-468-2319
Fax: 902-468-3666
5430 Highway 104, Westville, NS B0K 2A0
Telephone: 902-396-1800
Fax: 902-396-3360

Historic Houseparts
Vintage and reproductions: doors, windows,
stained glass, radiators, bath fixtures, plumbing,
lighting, mantels, hardware, cabinetry, shutters
540 South Avenue, Rochester, NY 14620
Telephone: 888-558-2329
Web site: www.historichouseparts.com

Horsefeathers Architectural Antiques
Doors, mantels, windows, stained glass, light-
ing, plumbing fixtures, columns, fencing,
gates, marble, stairway components, more
346 Connecticut Street, Buffalo, NY 14213
Telephone: 716-882-1581
Fax: 716-882-0215
Web site: www.horsefeathers-antiques.com
E-mail: horsefoe@buffnet.net

House of Antique Hardware
Door hardware & accessories: rare & ornate hard-
ware; antique styles; historic reproductions
3439 NE Sandy Blvd., P.M.B. #106, Portland, OR
97232
Telephone: 888-223-2545, 503-231-4089
Fax: 503-233-1312
Web site: www.houseofantiquehardware.com

Island Girl Salvage
Doors, windows, fireplace, lighting, bath and
kitchen, marble, garden elements, more
74 South Evergreen Way, Arlington Heights, IL
60005
Telephone: 847-392-2726
Web site: www.islandgirlsalvage.com
E-mail: Islandgirlsalvage@yahoo.com

Eron Johnson Antiques, Ltd.
Doors, fireplaces, capitals, fireplaces and
accessories, stained glass, windows, iron
doors/gates/arches/transoms, other architec-
tural pieces
451 Broadway, Denver, CO 80203
Telephone: 303-777-8700
Fax: 303-777-8787
Web site: www.antiques-internet.com
E-mail: eron@eronjohnsonantiques.com

King Richard's
Religious artifacts, including stained glass windows, lighting, marble products, more
1007 Union Center Drive, Alpharetta, GA 30004-5659
Telephone: 678-393-6500
Web site: www.kingrichards.com
E-mail: info@kingrichards.com

LASSCO—The London Architectural Salvage and Supply Co.
Flooring and timber, paneling, brasswork and lighting, radiators, bathroom fixtures and fittings, kitchen items, nautical fittings, ironwork, street furniture, pub bars and interiors, ecclesiastical woodwork, circus and fairground paraphernalia, more
Bermondsey, London South East
Telephone: +44 (0) 2073-942103
Website: www.lassco.co.uk

Legacy Building Supply
Doors, windows, bathroom fixtures, plumbing, mantels, fireplace items, radiators, staircases, stained glass, hardware, bricks, beams and reclaimed lumber, flooring
540 Division Street, Cobourg, Ontario
Telephone: 905-373-0796
Web site: www.legacybs.com

LooLoo Design
Antique plumbing fixtures and bath accessories
255 Bristol Ferry Road, Portsmouth, RI 02871
Telephone: 800-508-0022
Web site: www.looloodesign.com
E-mail: Jill@LooLooDesign.com

Marc Maison - Architectural and Garden Antiques
Doors, mantles, fireplaces, stained glass, room panels, tiles/pavers/stones, plumbing fixtures, stairs, garden antiques, more
178, rue du Faubourg Saint Honoré, 75008 Paris
Telephone: +33 (0) 1.76.90.15.28 Mobile (English): 06.60.62.61.90
Website: www.marcmaison.com
e-mail: marc-maison@wanado.fr
USA Contact: Simon Castle Antiques
11924 Vose St., North Hollywood, CA 91605
1-800-AGA-6070

Materials Unlimited
Doors, stained and beveled glass windows, mantels, restored lighting, furniture
2 West Michigan Avenue, Ypsilanti, MI
Telephone: 800-299-9462
Fax: 734-482-3636
Web site: www.materialsunlimited.com

Metropolitan Artifacts
Indoor and outdoor lighting, mantels, bathtubs and sinks, door hardware, iron and bronze items, garden ornamentation
4783 Peachtree Road, Atlanta, GA 30341
Telephone: 770-986-0007
Fax: 770-457-8670
Web site: www.metropolitanartifacts.com
E-mail: metartinc@aol.com

New England Architectural Center
Doors, mantels, hardware, stained and leaded glass, lighting, metalwork, vintage cobblestones, more
334 Knight Street, Warwick, RI 02886
Telephone: 401-732-1362
24 Franklin Street, Newport, RI 02840
Telephone: 401-845-9233

New England Demolition and Salvage
Doors, windows, radiators, claw-foot tubs, sinks, cabinets, hearths, shutters, columns
3065 Cranberry Highway, Unit 6, E. Wareham, MA 02538
Telephone: 508-291-7258
Web site: www.nedsalvage.com
E-mail: homeneds@aol.com

Nor'East Architectural Antiques
Doors, mantles, windows, lighting, plumbing, hardware, cabinetry, flooring and stair parts, more
14 Oakland Street, Amesbury, MA 01913
Telephone: 978-834-9088
Fax: 978-834-9089
Web site: www.noreast1.com
E-mail: mail@noreast1.com

Normandy Imports, Inc.
Antique French items: doors, mantels, chimney pots, antique wood, stone basins and tables
1102 Falls Road, Rock Hill, SC
Telephone: 803-328-9232
Web site: www.normandyimports.com
E-mail: normandyimports@aol.com

North Shore Architectural Antiques
Doors, windows, mantels, ceiling tin, lighting, electrical, plumbing and fixtures, tile, stone and pavers, columns, stairway components, more
521 7th Street, Two Harbors, MN 55616
Telephone: 218-834-0018
Web site: www.north-shore-architectural-antiques.com

Nutting House Antiques Center
Architectural and garden elements, decorative accessories
40 Park Street, Brandon, VT 05733
Telephone: 802-247-3302; 802-247-9452
Web site: www.nutting-house-antiques.com
E-mail: info@nutting-house-antiques.com

Ohmega Salvage General Store
Doors, windows, mantels, lighting, cabinets, hardware, decorative elements
2400 San Pablo Ave, Berkeley, CA 94702
Telephone: 510-204-0767
Fax: 510-843-7123
Web site: www.ohmegasalvage.com
E-mail: ohmegasalvage@earthlink.net

Old House Parts Company
Antique doors, windows, lighting, mantles, plumbing fixtures, stairway parts, hardware, reclaimed wood, garden elements and miscellaneous
24 Blue Wave Mall, Kennebunk, ME 04043
Telephone: 207-985-1999; Fax: 207-985-1911
Web site: www.oldhouseparts.com
E-mail: Parts@OldHouseParts.com

Olde Good Things (NY) (PA)
Reclaimed wood flooring, doors, windows, plumbing fixtures, mantels, stained glass, moldings, iron work, terra cotta, antique hardware, more
124 W. 24th Street, New York, NY 10011
Telephone: 212-989-8401
Fax: 212-463-8005
400 Gilligan Street, Scranton, PA 18508
Telephone: 570-341-7668
Web site: www.oldegoodthings.com
eBay store: oldegoodthings
E-mail: mail@oldegoodthings.com

Oliffs Architectural Antiques
Reclaimed items, no reproductions; Tudor, Georgian, Regency, Edwardian, Victorian. Fireplaces and surrounds, inserts, ranges, doors, doorways, windows, lighting, stained glass, wide oak floorboards, bathroom fittings and fixtures, hardware, garden and outdoor elements.
21 Lower Redland Road, Redland, Bristol, BS6 6TB
Telephone: +44 (0) 1179-239232
Website: www.oliffs.co,
e-mail: marcus@oliffs.com

Omega Too
Antique and reproduction lighting, custom Craftsman doors, medicine cabinets, hand made curtain rods
2204 San Pablo Ave., Berkley, CA 94702
(510) 843-3636

Orlando Liquidators, Inc.
New, used, antique and salvaged architectural and all sorts of building materials
1016 Savage Ct., Longwood, FL 32750
Telephone: 407-332-6206
Fax: 407-332-6208
Web site: www.orlandoliquidators.com
E-mail: info@orlandoliquidators.com

Pack Rat Architectural Salvage
Old wood/timber, flooring, barns, antique/used brick, doors, windows, lighting, mantles, hardware, stone, more
100 South Broadway Street, Providence, KY 42450
Telephone: 270-339-0879
Web site: www.packratsalvage.netfirms.com

Pieces of the Past
Doors, windows, hardware, stained glass, copper and iron items, garden, miscellaneous; sales and rentals
411 West Monroe, Austin, TX 78704
Telephone: 512-326-5141
Fax: 512-326-5181
Web site: www.pieces-of-the-past.com

Pinch of the Past
Antiques, reproductions, restoration, custom work. Hardware, lighting, plumbing, doors, columns, windows, shutters
109 W. Broughton Street, Savannah, GA 31401
Telephone: 912-232-5563
Fax: 912-232-5563
Web site: www.pinchofthepast.com
E-mail: pinchopast@aol.com

Pioneer Millworks
Reclaimed, custom milled woods—includes heart pine, ash, beech, chestnut, elm, hickory, maple, mixed oak, barn boards, jarrah, wine wood, more
1180 Commercial Drive, Farmington, NY 14425
Telephone: 585-924-9970, 800-951-9663
Fax: 585-924-9962
Web site: www.pioneermillworks.com
E-mail: valerie@pioneermillworks.com

Portland Architectural Salvage
Doors, windows, stained and leaded glass, mantels, stair parts, columns, shutters, plumbing, hardware, lighting, furniture, garden items, more
919 Congress Street, Portland, ME 04101
Telephone: 207-780-0634
Web site: www.portlandsalvage.com
E-mail: preserve@portlandsalvage.com

Quebec Aubaines Recycle
Reclamation Yard
207 rue Saint-Vallier Est, Quebec, QC, G1K 3P2, Quebec
Telephone: 418-529-8003

The RE Store
Doors, windows, plumbing fixtures, lighting, hardware, columns, radiators
1440 NW 52nd Street, Seattle, WA 98107
Telephone: 206-297-9119
Fax: 206-297-7260
Web site: www.re-sources.org
E-mail: seattle@re-sources.org
600 W. Holly Street, Bellingham, WA 98225
Telephone: 360-647-5921
Fax: 360-647-2948
E-mail: Restore@re-sources.org

Architectural Salvage Companies—by Name (continued)

Re Use the Past
Heartpine flooring and doors, ceiling tin, doors, windows, stained glass, lighting, hardware, bricks and pavers
98 Moreland Street, Grantville, GA 30220
Telephone: 770-583-3111
Web site: www.reusethepast.com
E-mail: bocastle@mindspring.com

Recycling The Past
Mantels, doors, columns, windows, stained glass, lighting fixtures, hardware, kitchen & bath, garden antiques, wrought iron, newel posts, gingerbread, molding, Victorian pieces, porches, tiles, more
381 North Main Street, Barnegat, NJ 08005
Telephone: 609-660-9790
Fax: 800-878-3251
Web site: www.recyclingthepast.com
E-mail: recycling@comcast.net

Renovators Resource, Inc.
Doors, windows, lighting, fireplace components, plumbing fixtures, stair components, wood flooring, timbers, hardware
6040 Almon Street, Halifax, Nova Scotia B3K 1T8
Telephone: 902-429-3889
Fax: 902-425-6795
Web site: www.renovators-resource.com

The ReStore
Habitat for Humanity
75 Archibald St, Winnipeg, R2J 0V7, Manitoba
Telephone: 204-233-5160
Fax: 204-233- 5198
120 Northfield Drive East, Waterloo, Ontario N2J 4G8
Telephone: 519-747-0664

Ricca's Architectural Sales
Doors, leaded and stained glass, fireplace components, shutters
511 North Solomon Street, New Orleans, LA 70119
Telephone: 504-488-5524
Web site: www.riccasarchitectural.com

Robinson's Antiques
Extensive antique hardware, mirror resilvering
763 West Bippley Road, Lake Odessa, MI 48849
Telephone: 616-374-7750
Web site: www.robinsonsantiques.com
E-mail: antiquehardware@robinsonsantiques.com

Salvage Heaven, Inc.
Doors, windows, lighting, electrical, tin ceiling, plumbing fixtures, fireplace components, flooring, moldings, wrought iron, bricks, pavers, more
206 East Lincoln Avenue, Milwaukee, WI 53207
Telephone: 414-482-0286
Fax: 414-482-0308
Web site: www.salvageheaven.com
E-mail: recycle@SalvageHeaven.com

Salvage Mill
Doors, windows, stained glass, mantels, vintage bathtubs, antique hardware
1 Lumber Lane, Manchester, NH 03102
Telephone: 603-622-0370
Web site: www.thesalvagemill.com
E-mail: thesalvagemill@cs.com

Salvage One
Doors, windows, mantels and accessories, plumbing fixtures, lighting, stairway parts, garden ornaments, barns, log cabins, out-buildings, lightning rods
1840 West Hubbard Street, Chicago, IL 60622
Telephone: 312-733-0098; Fax: 312-733-6829
Web site: www.salvageone.com
E-mail: staff@salvageone.com

Salvage Supermarket
12 acres: Doors, windows, plumbing, electrical, bath fixtures, lumber, more
1042 Oxford St. West, Winnipeg, Manitoba, R2C 2Z2
Telephone: 204- 222-2248
Fax: 204-224-4547
Web site: www.autobahn.mb.ca
E-mail: salvage@autobahn.mb.ca

Salvagewrights Ltd.
Doors, windows, mantels and accessories, plumbing fixtures, lighting, stairway parts, heating registers, garden ornaments and tiles
P.O. Box 1132, Orange, VA 22960
Telephone: 540-672-4456
Fax: 540-672-6822
Web site: www.salvagewrights.com
E-mail: info@salvagewrights.com

Santa Fe Wrecking Company
Doors, windows, plumbing fixtures, lighting, hardware, appliances, more
1600 South Santa Fe Ave, Los Angeles, CA 90021
Telephone: 213-623-3119
Web site: www.santafewrecking.com

Sattler's Stained Glass Studio, Ltd.
Repair, restoration, conservation, custom stained-glass pieces
RR1, Pleasantville, NS, Canada B0R 1G0
Telephone: 902-688-1156
Fax: 902-688-1475

Scotia Antique Wood
Reclaimed beams, planks, and boards, architectural antiques
Rod Fairn: 902-542-2075; fairn@scotiaantiquewood.com
Fritz Weiland: 902-542-0385; weiland@ns.sympatico.ca
Hugh McGoldrick: 902-582-3052
Web site: www.scotiaantiquewood.com

Seattle Building Salvage
Doors, windows, stained glass, lighting, plumbing fixtures, hardware, architectural house parts
330 Westlake Ave. N, Seattle, WA 98103
Telephone 206-381-3453
2114 Hewitt Avenue, Everett, WA 98201
Telephone: 425-303-8500
Fax: 425-783-0529
Web site: www.seattlebuildingsalvage.com

Second Renaissance Architectural Elements
Architectural salvage and artisan handcrafted architectural elements
1025 Wilson Avenue, Chambersburg, PA 17201
Telephone: 717-261-5708
Web site: www.secondrae.com
E-mail: bat@cvns.net

Second Use
Doors, windows, plumbing fixtures, cabinets, lighting, vintage molding, flooring, architectural details, hardware, miscellaneous
7953 2nd Avenue South, Seattle, WA 98108
Telephone: 206-763-6929
Web site: www.seconduse.com
E-mail: seattle@seconduse.com

Shaver Brothers
Doors, windows, hardware, porchposts, radiators, claw-foot bathtubs, sinks, shutters, hardwood flooring, corbels, stained glass windows, lighting, fencing, moldings, more. Custom millwork & restoration
eBay auctions
32 Perrine Street, Auburn, NY 13021
Telephone: 800-564-7206
Web site: www.shaverbrothers.com

Shiningwater Enterprises
Antique and used building materials, windows, doors, reclaimed flooring, stained glass
484 Mill Road, Lincoln, VT 05443
Telephone: 802-453-2825
Fax: 802-453-2825

Significant Elements
Windows, doors, plumbing fixtures, lighting, cabinetry, wood flooring and moldings, hardware, slate and ceramic tile, more
212 Center Street, Ithaca, NY 14850
Telephone: 607-277-3450
Fax: 607-277-4073
Web site: www.significantelements.org
E-mail: elements@lightlink.com

Simon's Hardware/Bath
Architectural and decorative hardware; bath, kitchen, and bar fixtures
421 3rd Avenue, New York, NY 10016
Telephone: 212-532-9220

Soll's Antiques
Doors, stained and beveled glass windows

Route 2, P.O. Box 307, Canaan, ME 04924
Telephone: 207-474-5396
Web site: www.antiquestainedglass.net
E-mail: solantiq@verizon.net

Southern Accents Architectural Antiques
Doors, antique entryways, beveled and stained glass, lighting, mantels, stairway components, bath fixtures, iron work, more
308 2nd Ave SE, Cullman, AL
Telephone: 205 737 0554
Web site: www.antiques-architectural.com
E-mail: info@antiques-architectural.com

Steptoe & Wife Architectural Antiques
90 Tycos Drive, Toronto, Ontario, M6B 1V9
Telephone: 416-780-1707; 800-461-0060
Fax: 416-780-1814
Web site: www.steptoewife.com
E-mail: info@steptoewife.com

TerraMai
Reclaimed solid wood from around the world: redwood siding, Douglas fir timbers, teak decking, hardwood flooring, more
P.O. Box 696, 1104 Firenze Street, McCloud, CA 96057
Telephone: 800-220-9062
Fax: 530-964-2745
Web site: www.terramai.com
E-mail: info@terramai.com

Timeless Classic Elegance
Antique leaded stained glass windows from the U.K.
3035 Barat Road, Montreal, Quebec, H3Y 2H8, Canada,
Web site: www.trocadero.com
E-mail: eserafini@timelessclassicelegance.com

Tony's Architectural Salvage
Doors, stained and beveled glass, plumbing fixtures, stone and marble statues, lighting, gates, fencing, grills, wood carvings, beams, windows, columns, staircases, mantels, hardware, more
123 N. Olive Street, Orange, CA 92866
Telephone: 714-538-1900
Fax: 714-538-1966
Web site: www.tonysarchitecturalsalvage.com
E-mail: thesalvageking@msn.com

Two Fraser Street
Antique and reproduction, furniture/accessories/architectural
2 Fraser Street, Shakespeare, ON N0B 2P0
Telephone: 519-625-882

Uncle John's Gingerbread Trim
Gingerbread trim, brackets, pendants, dormers, gables, spandrels, mouldings, screen door trim, more
5229 Choupique Road, Sulphur, LA 70665
Telephone: 337-527-9696

Architectural Salvage Companies–by Name

Uniquities Architectural Antiques
Chimney pots, antique stained and etched
  glass, finials, iron items, antique
  brick/stone/slate/tiles, salvaged wood flooring
5240 - 1a Street, SE Calgary, Alberta, T2H 1J1,
  Canada
Telephone: 403-228-9221
Fax: 403-283-9226
Web site: www.uniquities-archant.com
E-mail: info@uniquities-archant.com

United House Wrecking
Antiques and reproductions, European and
  American. Doors, mantels, stained glass,
  lighting, plumbing fixtures, garden elements,
  furniture
535 Hope Street, Stamford, CT 06906
Telephone: 203-348-5371
Fax: 203-961-9472
Web site: www.unitedhousewrecking.com

Vermont Salvage (MA)
75 Webster Street, Worcester, MA 01603
Telephone 508 755 2870

Vermont Salvage (NH)
Doors, radiators, plumbing, lighting, cabinetry,
  hardware, wrought iron fencing, mantels,
  French doors, stained glass windows
 2 Lumber Lane, Manchester, NH 03102
 Telephone: 603-624-0868
 Web site: www.vermontsalvage.com

Vermont Salvage (VT)
 Doors, radiators, plumbing, lighting, cabinetry,
  hardware, wrought iron fencing, mantel-
  pieces, French doors, stained-glass win-
  dows, lots more
 Gates Street, P.O. Box 453, White River
  Junction, VT 05001
 Telephone: 802-295-7616
 Web site: www.vermontsalvage.com

VictorianHardware.Com
Fine Victorian brass, bronze, and cast iron hard-
  ware and related antiques
P.O. Box 258, 20 Spahr Road, Washington, ME
  04574
Telephone: 207-845-2270
Web site: www.victorianhardware.com
E-mail: jspahr@pivot.net

Vintage Details, Ltd.
Demolition sales and salvage service
566 Prarie, Glen Ellyn, IL 60137
Telephone: 630-251-2329
Web site: www.vintagedetails.com

Vintage Plumbing
Victorian to Arts & Crafts American bath fixtures: Roman-style tubs, unusual toilets,
  pedestal sinks, rib-cage showers, unique
  accessories, foot baths, sitz baths; repair &
  replacement of broken or missing parts
Web site sales only
9645 Sylvia Ave., Northridge, CA 91324
Telephone: 818-772-1721
Web site: www.vintageplumbing.com
E-mail: vintageplumbing@sbcglobal.net

**White River Architectural Salvage and
Antiques**
Bars, benches, tile, doors, flooring, lighting, iron-
  work, plumbing fixtures, statuary, windows,
  more. Full service restoration company
1325 West 30th Street, Indianapolis, IN 46208
Telephone: 800-262-3389
Web site: www.whiteriversalvage.com

Wood Natural Restorations
Doors, windows, mantels, cupboards, cabinets,
  restored antique lumber, hardware, stone, log
  cabins, barns, outbuildings, vintage homes
  also available
3038 Woodlane Avenue, Orefield, PA 18069
Telephone: 610-395-6451
Web site: www.woodnatural.com

Canada

ALBERTA
Architectural Clearinghouse
Uniquities Architectural Antiques

BRITISH COLUMBIA
All Around Demolition Co Ltd.
Antique Market

MANITOBA
The Re-Store
NEW BRUNSWICK
Grindstone

NEWFOUNDLAND
Exploits Salvage

NOVA SCOTIA
Happy Harry's Used Building Materials
Renovator's Resource
Sattler's Stained Glass Studio, Ltd.
Scotia Antique Wood

ONTARIO
Artefacts
Balleycanoe and Co.
Door Store—Ontario
Legacy Building Supply
The Re-Store
Steptoe & Wife Architectural Antiques
Two Fraser Street

QUEBEC
Quebec Aubaines Recycle
Timeless Classic Elegance

SASKATCHEWAN
Auctionsales.ca

WINNIPEG
Salvage Supermarket

YUKON
Country Image Antiques

France

GRIMAUD
Les Matériaux du Littoral

HAUTE-SAVOIE
Antiques Forain

HOUDAN
Origines Architectural Antiquities

PARIS
Marc Maison—Architectural and Garden
  Antiques

TOURCOING
Architecture & Materiaux Authentiques

VILLENEUVE D'ASCQ
Rémy Motte

United Kingdom

BERMONDSEY, LONDON SOUTH EAST, ENGLAND
LASSCO—The London Architectural Salvage
and Supply Co.

CANTERBURY, KENT, ENGLAND
Bygones Architectural Reclamation

REDLAND, BRISTOL, ENGLAND
Oliffs Architectural Antiques

WEEFORD (NR LICHFIELD), STAFFORDSHIRE, ENGLAND
Blackbrook Antiques Village

WEST PARLEY, WIMBOURNE, DORSET, ENGLAND
Ace Demolitions Center

NEWTOWNARDS, CO DOWN, NORTHERN IRELAND
Ballyalton House

EDINBURGH, LOTHIAN, SCOTLAND
Edinburgh Architectural Salvage Yard

United States

ALABAMA
Architectural Antique Warehouse
Architectural Heritage
Southern Accents Architectural Antiques

ARKANSAS
Architectural Salvage by Ri-Jo

CALIFORNIA
Affordable Antique Bath & More
Amazing Glaze Restorations
Antiquarian Traders
Architectural Salvage (CA)
Crown City Hardware
DEA Bathroom Machineries
Doors Of London
Ohmega Salvage General Store
Santa Fe Wrecking Company
Tony's Architectural Salvage
Vintage Plumbing

COLORADO
Architectural Antiques (CO)
Architectural Artifacts (CO)
Belcour
Eron Johnson Antiques, Ltd.

CONNECTICUT
American Timbers, LLC
United House Wrecking

DISTRICT OF COLUMBIA
The Brass Knob
The Brass Knob's Back Doors Warehouse

FLORIDA
Allison's Architectural Antique Salvage
American Salvage, Inc.
Authentic Provence
Decodame.Com
Florida Victorian Architectural Antiques
Orlando Liquidators, Inc.

GEORGIA
Aardvark Antiques
Architectural Accents
Eugenia's Antique Hardware
Great Gatsby's
King Richard's
Metropolitan Artifacts
Pinch of the Past
Re Use the Past

ILLINOIS
Advanced Refinishing
Airport Lumber Company
Al Bar - Wilmette Platers
All the Things You Love
Architectural Artifacts, Inc. (IL)
Carlson's Barnwood Co.

Architectural Salvage Companies—by Location

ILLINOIS (continued)
Cook County Demolition Sales
Island Girl Salvage
Salvage One
Vintage Details, Ltd.

INDIANA
White River Architectural Salvage and Antiques

IOWA
Gavin Historical Brick

KENTUCKY
Architectural Salvage, W.D. Inc.
Pack Rat Architectural Salvage

LOUISIANA
Albany Woodworks
Architectural Salvage (LA)
Armadillo-South Architectural Salvage, Inc.
Crescent City Architecturals
Uncle John's Gingerbread Trim
Ricca's Architectural Sales

MAINE
Allie's Enterprizes
Architectural Antiquities
FIFI's House Parts and Salvage
Old House Parts Company
Portland Architectural Salvage

Soll's Antiques
VictorianHardware.Com

MARYLAND
DHS Designs

MASSACHUSETTS
Architectural Timber & Millwork
City Lights Antique Lighting
Good Time Stove Co.
New England Demolition and Salvage
Nor'East Architectural Antiques
Vermont Salvage (MA)

MICHIGAN
Materials Unlimited
Robinson's Antiques

MINNESOTA
Architectural Antiques (MN)
City Salvage—Architectural Salvage and
   Antiques
Duluth Timber Company
North Shore Architectural Antiques

MISSOURI
A & O Architectural Salvage
Cottage Castle Homes

NEBRASKA
A & R Salvage & Recycling, Inc.

NEW HAMPSHIRE
Admac Salvage
Architectural Salvage, Inc.
Blue Moon Salvage
Carlisle Wide Plank Floors
Salvage Mill
Vermont Salvage (NH)

NEW JERSEY
American Antique and Specialty Woods
Amighini Architectural, Inc.
Architectural Salvage and Antiques
Recycling The Past

NEW YORK
Architiques
Aurora Lampworks
Bedford Salvage Company
Cornerstone
Historic Houseparts
Horsefeathers Architectural Antiques
Olde Good Things (NY)
Pioneer Millworks
Shaver Brothers
Significant Elements
Simon's Hardware/Bath

NORTH CAROLINA
English Antique Imports

OHIO
Architectural Artifacts (OH)

OKLAHOMA
Architectural Elements

OREGON
Aurora Mills Architectural
House of Antique Hardware

PENNSYLVANIA
Aged Woods / Yesteryear Floorworks Co.
Architectural Antiques Exchange
Ball and Ball
The Chimney Pot Shoppe
Cityscape Properties
Ed Donaldson Hardware Restoration
Olde Good Things (PA)
Second Renaissance Architectural Elements
Wood Natural Restorations

RHODE ISLAND
LooLoo Design
New England Architectural Center

SOUTH CAROLINA
Carolina Architectural Salvage @ Cogan's
   Antiques
Normandy Imports, Inc.

TENNESSEE
Architectural Exchange
Garden Park Antiques

TEXAS
Adkins Architectural Antiques
Cunningham Lumber
Pieces of the Past

VERMONT
Architectural Salvage Warehouse (VT)
The Barn People
Nutting House Antiques Center
Shiningwater Enterprises
Vermont Salvage (VT)

VIRGINIA
Appalachian Woods Antique Flooring
Black Dog Salvage
Caravati's Inc.
Salvagewrights Ltd.

WASHINGTON
Chen Ragan, LLC
Earthwise
The RE Store
Seattle Building Salvage
Second Use

WISCONSIN
Salvage Heaven, Inc.